*Thoughts
for your
walk*

Thoughts for your walk

Joseph Kleman

Copyright © 2012 by Joseph Kleman.

Library of Congress Control Number: 2012908329
ISBN: Hardcover   978-1-4771-1003-4
               Softcover   978-1-4771-1002-7
               Ebook   978-1-4771-1004-1

All rights reserved. No part of this book may be reproduced or transmitted in any form or by any means, electronic or mechanical, including photocopying, recording, or by any information storage and retrieval system, without permission in writing from the copyright owner.

This book was printed in the United States of America.

To order additional copies of this book, contact:
Xlibris Corporation
1-888-795-4274
www.Xlibris.com
Orders@Xlibris.com

THOUGHT LIST

THOUGHTS

What Does God Want 15
    A look at what God really desires from you and me.
Rules 19
    Why God made rules and what are their purpose?
Chicken or the Egg 25
    Relationships—decision or emotion?
Guard Your Heart 29
    How well kept is your heart?
Hypocrisy 35
    Offends God, foundation of "religion", and your guilty!
Love vs. Judgment 43
    Fine line between the two, which side do you walk?
Love Your Enemy 47
    Confronting society as a Christian.
Stand Firm 53
    Facing the world as it exists today.
Conflict 57
    How do you deal with conflict in today's world?
Who Knows Best 61
    Do you really know and trust who is in charge?
Where's My Joy? 63
    Discovering where your joy really lies!
Celebrate the Victories 69
    What is your focus, victories or defeats?

SOME *REALLY* HEAVY THOUGHTS!

Acknowledged Man 75
   What does it mean to be an Acknowledged Man?
Prayer 81
   The basics of prayer.
Bible: Fact or Fiction 87
   Is the Bible true or not and where do you place it?
Salvation 91
   What does it mean to be "saved"?
Salvation Cautions 95
   If you *think* you're saved, you better read this!
Baptism 99
   Baptism as I have come to see it today.
Fasting 105
   What does it mean to "Fast"?
Questions of Purgatory 113
   My best explanation!
Speaking in Tongues 117
   What the Bible has to say!
Todays Sermon 127
   My message from *my* pulpit (no laughing)!

ARMOR OF GOD THOUGHTS
   An intense thought on what Paul writes in Ephesians!... 135

FINAL PRAYER
   Prayer for Spiritual Strength 153

FROM THE AUTHOR...

I want you to know, that my heart passionately leaps at the thought of you picking up this book; for that means that your relationship with your creator is already in your thoughts. I have come to firmly believe that no matter where you are in your Christian walk; your Heavenly Father is calling you to a deeper, more personal and more intimate relationship with Him. Whether you are a spiritual leader, a casual Christian, a weekly church attender, a new believer or a non-believer . . . God is calling you to greater relationship.

   I have such a desire; not only for you, but those around you to search out, call out, reach out to your Heavenly Father; for He is wanting, He is waiting, and He *is* calling.

   Please join me in my quest to share this message at *josephkleman.com*. We need to work together, to help each other to grow in our relationship with our Heavenly Father. As you grow in your relationship, I pray that the Holy Spirit will incite a passion for you to unite with me on a sole mission of igniting and reminding the world that . . . Your Father is calling!

   I thank-you for your heart and your support; I pray that the love and grace of Jesus Christ will bless you and those around you as you ponder and reflect on these thoughts, and that the Holy Spirit will guide you towards a deeper and more meaningful relationship with your Heavenly Father.

-Joseph P. Kleman

EXPLANATION

So you've picked up this book and you're wondering; "What's this all about?" First, I would like to personally thank-you for taking the time to pick it up (mouths to feed and all that you know).

Second, you are in a spiritual place. Perhaps you already have a relationship with Jesus Christ and you just want to spend some time in reflection. Or maybe you know about Jesus Christ and are at a place where you are asking yourself what that really means. Or you have recently come into a relationship with Jesus Christ and you have questions. **Or** perhaps you don't know jack about this "Jesus" person and you're just curious about what Christians are talking about. Whatever your place; this book is a place to start . . . and it's only the beginning!

My hope and my desire is that this book be a launching pad to start conversations, to draw you and the people around you into reflection, discussion and meditation; all with the sole mission to bring you to an understanding that your Heavenly Father is calling for you.

Some will laugh at its simplicity; that's ok, I'm a simple person. Some will disagree with what I've said, been married 20 years—I'm used to being wrong. But whatever your reaction is . . . know this; that your walk is not your own, your life is temporary, your decisions have consequences, and your Father is waiting.

HOW TO USE THIS BOOK

I wrote this book to be informational, inspirational, and maybe entertaining; but most importantly, this book was written to **ignite thought.** This book is a collection of thoughts, more specifically my thoughts. Thoughts that have been brought about by my own struggles as well as in assisting those around me walk through theirs. I have written this book with the hopes and intentions that it be used in a variety of ways:

- Use the "Thought List" to identify specific subject matter.
- To be used as a devotional.
- To be used as a guide for small group discussion.
- To be a conversation starter.
- To be a beginning resource for new or young Christians.
- **To be shared.**

I pray these short, simple thoughts create an enhanced understanding and hunger for your own personal relationship with your Heavenly Father, His son Jesus Christ and the Holy Spirit. I also pray that you be inspired to not only read this book, but to share this book with those around you. I pray that this book arouses thought, reflection and conversations that light in you a passion for a greater relationship with our Heavenly Father and a greater ability to share that relationship with others!

May God bless you, fill you, strengthen and inspire you as we share together in my; "Thoughts for your walk".

THOUGHTS

WHAT DOES GOD WANT?

A simple question, what does God want? What does he want from us, what are His desires for me? The more time that I have spent on this "simple question", the more complicated it seemed. What does the Creator of the Universe want with me? Theologians, philosophers, great men of knowledge could probably spend days and even weeks speaking on the subject. Countless books have been written, page after page, chapter after chapter; but I believe I can sum it up in just a few short paragraphs. (Aren't I the confident one?!)

Every time I come to a question of the character of God, I quickly become overwhelmed. How do I attempt to understand God, to understand the character of God? It has been helpful for me to imagine God in a context that I can understand. The words of Jesus have been most useful when he attempted to teach us a format or content of prayer. In Matthew chapter 6, Jesus tried to give us an understanding of prayer, one of the most impactful parts of that lesson for me came in verse 9 when he referred to God as "Our Father".

> *Jesus instructed us to pray, referring to God as "Our Father".*
> Matthew 6:9

Having children myself, I have only just begun to get an understanding of God our Father. God our Father, the perfect Father . . . the **PERFECT** Father; the one who created us, the one who looks after us. The one who guides us, protects us, disciplines us, the one who waits for us.... Father.

I have read many books from a variety of authors. All have provided great insight on the character of God. I have also found that there are countless books on how to find the plan that God has for us, to live up to our Christian potential, to be better followers of Christ. I don't want to discredit, minimize or make light of any of these books or their authors. I have found every one of them to be very helpful and enlightening. They have been of great benefit to me in my own Christian walk and I recommend reading them. I just think that sometimes, we can get so enthusiastic about getting people on the right path; we forget to acknowledge the foundation of the road or the reason for the journey.

> *In our effort to "lead people to Christ", we forget to show them the love of Christ!*

Those who don't know Christ, see the road (following Christ) as a chore, a list of do's and don'ts. Non-believers see Christianity as one major guilt trip or God as a supernatural control freak that brings nothing but shame and limitations. New Christians get so caught up in their desire to travel "the path", it becomes an endless stream of service and performance in an attempt to get closer to God through works, through acts, by earning and achieving; caught up in an unfulfilled search for God's plan; not God's heart.

So what does God want then? The answer is simply a relationship. God wants a relationship with you. Sure He wants you to succeed, He has a plan for your life, He has wants and desires for you, He wants you to have success. But whether you follow His plan, have success, prosper or fail, your perfect Father wants a relationship with you! As a father myself, I have desires for my children. But know that my greatest earthly desire, no matter whether they succeed or fail,

> *Your Heavenly Father just wants a relationship with you.*

achieve or make mistakes; my desire is to have a relationship with my children and through that relationship, I hope to guide them, direct them, encourage them and I will love them regardless of what they do or what they become.

How much more would the perfect Father in Heaven desire a relationship with you? Search out God's plan for your life; but do it always in the context of desiring a deeper relationship with your Father. "Delight yourself in the Lord, and He will give you the desires of your heart." (Psalms 37:4) Your Father will be overjoyed in your service, in your achievements, in your desire to follow Him; but first He seeks your heart, He seeks a relationship.

For God **so loved the world**, that he gave his only Son, that whoever believes in him should not perish but have eternal life. For God did not send his Son into the world to condemn the world, but in order that the world might be saved through him. (John 3:16-17 ESV)

God so loved YOU, He sent His only beloved son; to be ridiculed, tortured and murdered; so that through Him, your eternal place in Heaven *with your Father* would be secured. Sin is simply anything that offends or separates you from your relationship with your Heavenly Father. Jesus Christ paid the price, the atonement for your sin; so that through HIM, you can freely engage in a relationship with your Heavenly Father. ***That*** is love. That is willing to sacrifice much to have a relationship with YOU!

Serve Him, work for Him; but never forget to spend time with Him. Don't let a day go by without time in prayer and in His Word. For only through spending time with Him does your relationship grow; don't, and your relationship WILL perish. God's laws are absolute. Don't spend time with your wife, your marriage will die. Don't spend time with your Father and that relationship too will die.

I pray that your true heart's desire is to have a deeper relationship with God your Father and that as your relationship grows; so does your understanding of your purpose. May the grace, peace and love of Jesus Christ bring you to a closer relationship with God, your perfect Father.

Go now . . . your Father is calling!

I WAS THINKING . . .

Is my Heavenly Father seeking my "right" behavior or my heart?

Am I trying to *earn* a relationship or *build* a relationship?

In truth, does my Heavenly Father looking to punish me or to love me?

Does God want me "in line" or in relationship?

RULES

"YEAH, SO WHY ARE THERE SO MANY RULES?"

I've heard all the excuses. "But if I become a Christian, I won't be able to have any fun anymore." "What's with all these commandments, can't I just live my own life?" "It's just too strict; I can't follow all these rules."

I know there are so many people out there with the misconception that being a Christian is nothing more than following a list of "do's and don'ts". If you're willing to open your mind a little, let me see if I can change your perspective a little bit.

So why are there rules and laws? Some are given to protect you: Don't run with scissors. Get good grades or you're grounded. Be in before ten. Some are given to protect you and the society that you exist in: Drive the speed limit. Don't steal. Don't kill anybody.

Righteous are you, O LORD, and right are your rules.
(Psalm 119:137 ESV)

All rules, especially those laid down by our Heavenly Father, are there not only to let you know what he expects and how you can honor Him; but they exist to protect you. Let's look at how a parent lay's down rules to protect their young.

You don't let your toddler climb on things so they won't fall and hurt themselves. You don't let your children play with dangerous items so they won't hurt themselves. You monitor your teenager's activities to try to prevent them from getting into situations where they can be . . . hurt! As parents we have a desire to protect our children.

As a society, we lay down law's to protect that society. There are social laws that prevent chaos and social breakdown; such as laws against theft and violence. We have traffic laws that exist to keep everyone who drives on the roads as safe as possible.

So how much more do you think your Heavenly Father who is perfect, and has nothing but a perfect love for you, wants to protect and keep you safe? Think about it, there is not one rule or commandment in the Bible that is not there but for your protection.

> *If you obey the commandments of the Lord your God that I command you today, by loving the Lord your God, by walking in his ways, and by keeping his commandments and his statutes and his rules, then you shall live and multiply, and the Lord your God will bless you (Deuteronomy 30:16)*

Let's go back to our parenting and social laws. These laws all exist to provide you an umbrella of protection. Obeying your parents does not guarantee that you will not get hurt, but by disobeying your parents, your risk of injury greatly compound. By not speeding, that is no guarantee that you will never be in an accident; but by breaking the law, it greatly compounds your risk of getting into an accident. Speeding puts others at risk as well so there is a punishment associated if caught violating the law. Drinking and driving greatly compounds your risk of hurting yourself or someone else.

> *You have commanded your precepts to be kept diligently. Oh that my ways may be steadfast in keeping your statutes! Then I shall not be put to shame, having my eyes fixed on all your commandments. I will praise you with an upright heart, when I learn your righteous rules. I will keep your statutes; do not utterly forsake me! (Psalm 119:4-8 ESV)*

You step outside the law; you greatly compound your risk of injury. You live your life inside the law; you are not guaranteed a perfect life, but one with much less risk of pain. The spiritual laws (God's laws) are no different. You violate his laws and guidance; you step outside the protection that it provides.

Look at the Ten Commandments. Each one exists as a guide to a life of a lot less stress and pain.

1. Worship any other Gods and He cannot and will not protect you!
2. Curse your God and again; He cannot and will not protect you!
3. A day of rest is needed for spiritual and physical renewal; do not honor this and your mind, body and spirit will suffer from exhaustion and neglect!
4. Honoring your parents is the best way to show honor to your Heavenly Father; if you cannot respect them, how can you respect Him!
5. Murder (don't make me explain this one)!
6. Adultery (again, if you cannot see the pain this brings on all involved, I'll never be able to explain it to you)!
7. Theft (self-explanatory)!
8. Lying (really)!
9. And 10. Coveting: Coveting leads you to greed. Coveting leads you to never being content with what you have. Coveting leads you to desiring what is not good for you. Coveting leads you down a path of unfulfilled hopes and desires that will leave you broken and never satisfied.

You need to grasp the concept that becoming a Christian, becoming a follower of Christ is not about a list of do's and don'ts; it is an understanding and a recognition that there is a greater force out there that is truly concerned for you, concerned for your happiness and desires for you the utmost joy in life.

God, through His son Jesus Christ, is offering you not a life of limitations, but a life of freedom. A life free from the pain and suffering that comes from living outside the protection that the laws and guidelines of the Bible provide.

You need to get this! God does not want to limit you, He wants to free you! Free you from the pain, free you from the suffering, and free you from the bondage that comes when you live outside His protection!

You are not called to give up your fun; you are called to give up the consequences of your "fun". (You might want to read that again!) The Bible warns in multiple books not to get drunk; I've never met anyone who violated that law and didn't truly regret it the next morning! Whether you accept it or not, life is about choices and consequences. Choosing to ignore the consequences does not negate the consequences for living outside the "rules".

An athlete is not crowned unless he competes according to the rules.
(2 Timothy 2:5 ESV)

Listen to me very carefully; it is not about following the rules, it's about following your heart. Don't worry, focus, or concentrate on the rules. Concentrate on finding a relationship with the one who created you and loves you beyond description. It is in that relationship and love where you will find yourself obedient to the "rules". Not out of being legislated, but out of a love so great you can't help but want to "follow the rules" and live in obedience with a heart that desires to please your creator, your ruler, your Heavenly Father.

I WAS THINKING . . .

Are the rules from the Bible that are passed down from God instituted to control me or are they given out of love and a desire to protect me . . . mostly from myself?

Do I want to follow His rules out of strict obedience; or do I have a heart that loves and respects my Heavenly Father and I truly desire to please and serve Him?

Do I fear the rules or do I have a greater fear of the thought of something greater than myself?

CHICKEN OR THE EGG

I was engaged in a conversation where a woman was talking of her boyfriend's struggle to "get saved". She had said he was waiting for it to "feel right". He was waiting for the Holy Spirit and then he would make his decision when the feeling was right. Immediately, alarms started going off in my head. I wasn't quite sure why that just didn't sound right.

This conversation led me into several days of prayer and reflection over what had been said. The thought that started me off was contemplating the foundation of relationships. Not just our relationship with our Heavenly Father, but the relationships around us. What about the foundation of relationships in marriage? What about the relationships with our children or our parents?

Emotions may spark a relationship, but they cannot sustain it

The relationship we engage in on a daily basis; could these be based on purely a feeling, on an emotion? I began to ponder the emotional question. Do I have a relationship today with my parents based on my feelings? The answer is no. I, like most children, have at times in my life harbored anger and resentment towards my parents, even blaming them for my "lot in life". What about my children? It is certainly not my feelings that have kept them around

Our heart is a selfish, self-serving, schizophrenic, bi-polar, angry, bitter, controlling, devious, deceiving, egomaniacal, misleading, misguiding creature

all this time. Heck, if based on feelings, I would have killed them both years ago! (That was a joke—lighten up.) What about my wife? Is my relationship with her based on how we felt before we got married? (Give me a second to compose myself after that one. I don't want to say that I got a giggle out of that, but I think I pulled a something.)

So is it purely about a decision then? Or is it the other end of the spectrum? Do I love all these people simply because I chose to, and now I'm stuck with them so I might as well love them? Is it both? Is it an emotion *or* a decision; or a decision *and* an emotion? And if it's both; which one comes first? Is it a decision that leads to an emotion or an emotion that leads to a decision? Is it the chicken or the egg?

As you can tell, it was a very thoughtful time for me. And even though I suffered through a few headaches and just utter confusion; I believe that God has revealed to me some of the answers to these questions. I hope that I can successfully share with you what has been laid upon my heart.

> *It must be a decision to a lifelong commitment that is the foundation of a marriage. And out of that a deeper, truer, more concrete emotional bond can be built. If not, it is superficial and temporary.*

First we have to identify the players in this chess match. I have been reading, and have written, on the condition of our heart. Let me tell you, as simply as I can what I have discovered about this precious organ. Our heart is a selfish, self-serving, schizophrenic, bi-polar, angry, bitter, controlling, devious, deceiving, egomaniacal, misleading, misguiding creature. (Feel free to read that again.) Our heart, and the desires of our heart, is as easily swayed and more easily manipulated than a donkey chasing a carrot. Why do you think so much money is spent today on and by advertisers? Because our hearts and our desires are so easily manipulated!

Let me point out to you what happens when me make decisions based on emotions. We buy a car that's too big, a house that's too big and a spouse that's too big! (Again, feel free to take a moment.) If we enter into a relationship and make a decision to get married based on an emotion; when that emotion changes, and it will, so will our decision. Let me take that a step farther, to where this concept really smacked me in the back of the head. If we make a decision to follow Christ based purely on an emotion, when that emotion fades, and it will, we will change our decision to follow Christ and fall away. Let me just stop there and tell you that I was on my motorcycle on my way to work and nearly wrecked as I broke into tears as that revelation hit me. There are so many times when my feelings or my "heart" was hurt by a church, a pastor, or as I perceived by "God"; and I would turn my back and walk away.

So this is what I have now come to believe. Our spouses and/or the Holy Spirit can prompt us, or get our attention with an emotional feeling. However; I have come to believe that it must be a decision that has to guide our emotions. Let me explain; it must be a decision to a lifelong commitment that is the foundation of a marriage. And out of *that decision*; a deeper, truer, more concrete emotional bond can be built. If not, it is superficial and temporary.

The same is true with our relationship with our Heavenly Father. It is only through a decision to commit to an eternal relationship that lays the foundation for an emotional bond that is deep, true, sincere, endless and unbreakable.

What if Noah *felt* stupid and didn't build the arc. What if Joseph *felt* abandoned and didn't stay faithful while in slavery in Egypt? What if Abraham *felt* betrayed and refused to sacrifice Isaac? What if Moses *felt* scared and didn't go to Egypt to free the Israelites? What if Jesus *felt* selfish and said; "I'm not going through that for them"? What if the disciples *felt* . . . and decided not to follow Jesus? If all of those mentioned made a decision based on a feeling; not only would history be different, but imagine the impact those decisions would have had on their relationship with their Heavenly Father? See what the impact has had in making a decision *for* their Heavenly Father!

Where would we spend eternity if we live in our feelings; if we *feel* too unworthy, too frightened, too doubtful, or too selfish to make the decision to accept Christ as our savior and enter into a relationship with our Heavenly Father? Our life is about a relationship. Not one based on emotion, but one founded in a decision; a decision from which the greatest love and the greatest relationship can be discovered.

May God grant us the strength, the courage, and the wisdom to stand firm in our decision to be faithful to the greatest relationship, the greatest love, the purest emotion; to the great "I AM" . . . Yahweh . . . Abba . . . Father.

I WAS THINKING . . .

Are my personal relationships (spouse, children, family, friends, etc.) based and grounded on my feelings towards them or my commitment to them?

Is my relationship with my Heavenly Father built on a feeling or built on a decision of a commitment?

As I look at the world around me; are relationships dwindling and failing due to lack of feelings or lack of commitment?

GUARD YOUR HEART

I was visiting a very old friend of mine. He's not old, just our friendship. I attended the church where he is a Youth Pastor and sat in on their Sunday Bible Study. The man teaching was talking about "guarding your heart". Initially, I was attentive but really not getting anything out of what he was saying. Then the Spirit hit me. I began to get a very powerful image that I want to share with you.

I began to get an image of a bank vault. Picture it in your head, back behind closed doors. Maybe you have to take an elevator to get to it. Perhaps pass through an iron gate and a metal detector to get to the vault. Guard standing in front of it, maybe two more out in the bank lobby, and a huge steel door with a ship steering wheel as a big lock. You know the image, you've seen them yourself or in a movie. *"Ocean's 11"* comes to mind for me! I want you to take a minute and really allow that image to evolve in your head and then allow me to start to input some thoughts into those images.

Let's start to think of the contents of our vault. If I had something of value that I wanted to preserve and protect, I would place it in a safe, maybe the bank or safety deposit box. What kind of things do I have that I would want to make that secure? What kind of things, if I had them, would I want to be guarded in a vault, a bank of that level of security? I wouldn't empty my trash and take it

Is my heart a vault or a junk drawer?

to a bank for safekeeping. Would I take my old dirty underwear to the bank and ask to sign it in? What things would I hold to be precious, irreplaceable, what things of great value would I want in my vault?

In addition, what measures would I take to keep the contents of the vault from becoming contaminated? Would I trust a vault that wasn't fireproof . . . waterproof? Would I want someone to put his or her old stinking socks in a drawer under my rare butterfly collection? Would I allow anything into my vault that was perhaps contaminated, poisoned or infested with disease or insects? Do you know what a goat could do to a stack of money? No goats in my vault!

What would the inside of your vault look like?

Now let's imagine for a minute, that our heart was our vault. What do we allow into our vaults? What elements of everyday life do we allow into our safe, our heart, our spirit, our soul? Is your vault full of anger and bitterness or does your, "heart overflow with pleasing themes" (Ps 45:1)? Are your deposits to your vault full of garbage or do you fill your vault with things of value, things to be treasured?

"I have stored up your word in my heart, that I might not sin against you." (Ps 119:11).

"My son, be attentive to my words; incline your ears to my saying. Let them not escape from your sight; keep them within your heart. For they are the life to those who find them, and healing to all their flesh. Keep your heart with all vigilance, for from it flow the springs of life. Put away from you crooked speech, and put devious talk far from you." (Proverbs 4:20-24)

> *Keep your heart with all vigilance, for from it flow the springs of life.*

What do you put in your vault? What is it you value, what is it you **should** treasure? What do the contents of your vault say about you? What do you treasure, what do you value, what do you hold sacred? What are you putting in your vault?

"As in water face reflects face, so the heart of a man reflects the man." (Proverbs 27:19). I have to tell you, in researching this, that last one hit me so hard my teeth hurt!

I, and I think anyone could spend years discussing what the contents of our hearts should be, but for the purpose of our conversation, I just wanted to start you thinking about what it is that is in your heart and what you should be guarding.

Well, I suppose that if we are guarding something, if we have something that we want protected, that we are obviously concerned about loss. If we weren't concerned about something being taken, we would not lock it up. So the first question I would ask if I were someone in charge of security. What am I protecting? What am I protecting it from? (Long pause for effect.) We all have to acknowledge that there is a thief that is bent on robbing us not only of our eternal salvation, but of any joy that we could have while here in the flesh. We need the grace of Jesus and the protection of the Holy Spirit to guard our vaults, "and give no opportunity to the devil. Let the thief no longer steal" (Ephesians 4:27-28). Paul warned Timothy to, "guard the deposit entrusted to you." (1 Timothy 6:20)

"Thorns and snares are in the way of the crooked, whoever guards his soul will keep far from them." (Proverbs 22:5) *Selah*

The next part of our discussion of guarding our heart is discussing who is standing guard over the entrance of our vault? Who do we have installing our lock, who is in charge of our security, who is at the door monitoring what goes in, and what comes out? We must trust in and enlist Jesus Christ and the Holy Spirit to be in charge of the security of our vault. There is none other for the job, and no other that I

Create in me a clean heart, oh God, and renew a right spirit within me.

would trust. We need to be vigilant in our effort to make sure that the security to our vault is in place daily.

"So we do not loose heart. Though our outer nature is wasting away, our inner nature is being renewed day by day." (1 Timothy 4:16)

We must have God the Father, His son Jesus Christ and the Holy Spirit in constant thought and prayer so that the thief does not get his opportunity.

"Create in me a clean heart, oh God, and renew a right spirit within me." (Psalms 51:10)

There is one more thing that I want you to consider in the use of your vault or your bank. If you had obtained something of value, and had taken the time to get it secured in your safe, and made sure that the appropriate guard was on duty. Would you not be very wise in how you would care for and invest your valuable possessions? So I suggest to you. That if you want your precious possessions, your valued treasures to remain secure and to have an opportunity to grow, you should want to invest it, and invest it wisely. You would not take your retirement and place it in risky investments with a chance of losing it all. You would take time to research, and with careful thought, consideration and planning (prayer), you would make sound decisions for solid investments. So think about what investments you should be making with your time, with your thoughts and with your heart so that the treasures God has given to you will grow. Read the parable of the talents, Matthew 25:14-30. A man gives 3 servants talents, 2 servants double what they had been given for the master; the third buried his in fear. Jesus tells of investing the gifts that we have been given and the consequences of poor choices.

Allow me to leave you with this final thought. "Do not lay up for yourselves treasures on earth, where moth and rust destroy and where thieves break in and steal, but lay up for yourselves treasures in heaven, where neither moth nor rust destroys and where the thieves do not break in and steal. **For where your treasure is, there your heart will be also.**" (Matthew 6:19-21)

I WAS THINKING . . .

What am I exposed to, or better yet—what do I allow myself to be exposed to, on a regular basis that contaminates my heart?

Do I protect my mind, my spirit and my heart or are my doors unlocked and standing wide open for "the thief"?

What have I put in my heart, and as a result what has come out?

HYPOCRISY

You know when you just say the word, I begin to conjure up all kinds of negative images and memories of negative encounters that I have had with "Christians", "religious" people, or the church. I immediately begin to regale myself in stories of all the "evil" people that I have encountered that also "align" themselves with God. Christians who just can't wait to smack you over the head with the Bible or with their own Christianity, yet clearly do not practice what they preach. What a bunch of, well . . . . hypocrites!

After a while, one begins to wonder; are all of these people evil? Are they all just tools of the devil sent to every church I go to with the sole intent of frustrating me and just ticking me off? Why would God allow such people in His church? Were they ever saved? Are they just evil? The more I question, the more I have questions. So being the answer driven person that I am, I began to ponder.

I started with the question, who are we in God's eye. The best place to answer that is the great resource (talking about the Bible, stay with me). After God had created the world and all that was in it, he beheld it and said it was "very good" (Gen 1:31). The Bible also says that we are created in his image (Gen 1:26), and that "everything created by God is good" (1 Tim 4:4). So that has lead me to the conclusion that in our creation, in our conception, that we are all basically "good".

So how do a people of a basic "good" nature, who are attempting to follow as God has planned, to live in His word (Bible again), and by His example (Jesus Christ), in a community by His design (church), get it so wrong. The church by its nature is not evil. The people who attend church, for the most part, have a true heart to follow Christ. So what in the world is going on! (There's a pun there.)

I have come up with some answers to the questions that may help you with your walk with Christ and perhaps help to prevent hypocrisy in your life. Maybe, if you are better able to understand the why and how hypocrisy occurs, you can be better able to prevent it from happening in your life, and to also help you to better identify, cope with, and address when it occurs in your church.

Ok . . . foundation. Before you can tackle any question related to God or religion, you have to have some basic understandings: There is a God, there is a devil; there is good and there is evil. The devil has been around since the beginning of our time. Since the temptation in the garden, to tempting Christ in the desert and his influence is ever expanding and growing to this day. If you don't understand that there is an active force in this world that will stop at nothing to derail you from your path to God, you are already deceived and will always come back to the question, "why". "For we do not wrestle against flesh and blood, but against the rulers, against the authorities, against the cosmic powers over this present darkness, against the spiritual forces of evil in the heavenly places." (Ephesians 6:12) So now that you at least have recognition of the spiritual struggle, we can begin to lay the foundation to understanding the "why".

So we are created to be good, we have an evil force fighting against us, but why is it so hard? Easy, a loving God that gave us choice. If all we had to choose from was good, how is their free will? If we go to a buffet and all that is available is beans and carrots, we would live very healthy, but have no

> *Free will is the choice between good and evil; accepting or rejecting God.*

choice. There is no free will until someone throws some grease, fat and deserts on the bar. Now I have a choice, now I can exercise my free will. (If you can wrap your brain around that, you are much further than most philosophers.) If you choose a more theological explanation; due to original sin, we are all born with a sinful nature with expectations to fail. "For all have sinned and fall short of the glory of God," (Rom 3:23). And we are also given the "out" to be completely forgiven for all those sins, "and are justified by His grace as a gift, through the redemption that is in Christ Jesus" (Rom 3:24). Whichever explanation works best for you, understand that sin is part of this world, it is all around us and it is in us. "If we say we have no sin, we deceive ourselves, and the truth is not in us." (1Johnn 1:8) Jesus promised the disciples when he said, "Temptations to sin are sure to come." (Luke 17:1). If you choose to believe that sin is not ever present, you are as the ostrich with its head in the sand. He thinks that he is hidden and no one can see him. "Did you ever notice that if you stick your head in the sand standing up, you present a tempting target to the devil?" (Mike Warnke)

Here we are, created as "good", with a nature to sin against God, and an invisible force that is giving us kidney punches. A force that is Hell bent (if you'll pardon another pun) on frustrating you right out of Heaven. If you have been a Christian for a while, this is not news to you. If you are new to being a Christian and this is new to you, please sit down and breathe before your brain melts! Being reminded of the "why's" in life can help to put some things into perspective. And to all the junior philosophers out there, there is absolutely more to understanding all the whys, but for our intent and purposes, let's roll over before we attempt to crawl or walk, shall we?

Now for the how . . . what's the hook, how are we so easily manipulated and pulled so far off course. Once you identify the "hook", you can begin to avoid the bait. (Using fishing reference here . . . by the way, we're the fish.) There are many different lures, hooks, baits and traps the devil uses to draw us off course, to get us into his nets. If I can show a few of them to you, the waters might start to look a little easier to navigate.

I would like to start with the word expectation. When you hear the word, "Christian", what images do you conjure up, what do you envision, what are your expectations? Before you became a Christian, what were your expectations? Did you hold Christians up to an unreasonably high standard? Did you hold Christians up to standards that you now realize, as a Christian, were unreasonable?

I have to admit, there was a time in my life, that all I did was look for the dirt, the chink in the armor. Introduce yourself as a Christian and I was going to find your flaw just to prove to you (and maybe myself) what a hypocrite you were. I would walk into a church, eyes wide open, ears at full tilt, mind in tuned to every movement, every sound; observing the placement of every item in the church, the moods and the attitudes of each and every person present; dissecting every word spoken or preached. I would not leave until I had revealed your "hypocrisy". Were my standards maybe just a little too high, did I perhaps expect perfection out of a world that well . . . . isn't. So who was the hypocrite?

Hypocrisy is first spotted by a hypocrite.

Expectations—I had the great honor and privilege to lead a woman to Christ. I would love to take credit, but I was just a lowly tool with Christ driving the hammer. It took a lot of chiseling to convince this woman that she needed Christ in her life. Interestingly enough, one of her hang-ups was . . . expectations. Not any expectations that I had placed on her; and certainly not any expectations placed by God or

Disappointment doesn't exist without expectation.

his son Jesus Christ. But she was hung up on the unreasonable expectations she had placed on herself. She didn't believe that she could make what she perceived to be the necessary behavioral modifications to become a Christian. She didn't think she could "act" the part. She didn't believe that she could meet the behavioral expectations that she perceived others would place on her, just by accepting Christ! The thing that was preventing here from coming to Jesus was an unreasonable, perceived expectation of how she would have to behave. REALLY!! Now hang on to this, it is going to become very important shortly.

One more time: Good people, with good intentions, and an evil force at the ready, with unreasonable expectations . . . what's next. In walks pride arm in arm with perception. (For those of you that didn't just throw this down and walk out of the room, I will go on.) Pride (pause again allowing word to soak in . . . .). Pride is like salt in that just a sprinkle and it's not too bad. Another sprinkle and the next thing you know; clogged arteries, hypertension, heart attack, stroke and death. (How many of you just thought about your salt intake . . . hmmm.) "It was just a sprinkle more . . ." read the epitaph! (I know I'm hitting close to home but stick with me.) Pride is not a bad thing. Pride is what makes you bathe everyday . . . . and we all thank you. Pride is what causes us to do well in school or compete well in sports. Pride is what keeps your home nice (maybe), or keeps you from littering the streets or the church. Pride in proper context is not a bad thing. However, the Bible comes with some very strict warnings: "Pride and arrogance are the way of evil" (Proverbs 8:13). "Pride goes before destruction" (Proverbs 16:18). "One's pride will bring him low."(Proverbs 23:23). Jesus talks very plainly in Mark 7:14-23 about what defiles a person. Pride is right in there.

But what does that have to do with perception? I'm glad you asked. I have worked in several fields. Different jobs and careers that I have invested much time and PRIDE into becoming somewhat of an expert in my field. I was good at what I did, I knew my job and I did it well. Nothing—and I mean nothing would anger me faster than for someone to challenge my abilities in my job. I was good, I worked hard to be good and I wanted to be perceived as someone that was good at what I did. Bad characteristics, perhaps not, after all, what is wrong with wanting to be good at what you do? Doesn't God promise to bless the fruits of your labor? But what if I'm not as good as I want to be perceived? What if I stretch the truth of what my abilities really are? I worked as a nurse, what's wrong with wanting my patients to have confidence in me? I should want them to trust me, to look to me. That's what I'm there for, right? What's wrong with telling a patient I'm really good at starting an IV, then, three needle sticks later and I'm going for help! Has that patient just judged me as a hypocrite? Are they judging the whole department, or perhaps the hospital? "Don't go there; they can't even start an IV!" Perception!

We all want to be the best we can be. We all want to try to walk in the footsteps of Jesus. We all have, or should have a desire to be the best Christians we can be. We should all want to grow in our understanding of what it means to be a Christian. However, we all have sinned, we all struggle with pride. We all want to be the best we can be, or at least to be *perceived* as being . . . . and there it happens.

We dress a little nicer because we don't want anyone to know our financial struggles. We force on a smile before getting to church to hide the hurt we have from our everyday lives. In an effort to deflect our own shortcomings, we quickly point out everyone else's problems so that maybe, no one will see where we have fallen short. So no one will see that we are struggling. Oh no, if they

> *I've been yelled at by a patient with a sprained ankle for making them wait; after having to tell a young mother her child died in a car crash.*
> *-perception*

see my struggles, then they will doubt my faith, they will doubt my beliefs. They will doubt my Christianity! So there it is, now I have painted on the veil of hypocrisy. Not in an effort to hurt, not to cause pain or to push people away from me, the church, or away from Christ, but in an attempt to hide, in an attempt to cover my own shortcomings, my own *perceived* failures.

We all have done it. How many times have you seen a fellow church member struggle, and instead of offering a hand, we offer judgment. Have we seen someone that may be hurting and just question their decisions or gossip about their struggles? Have you known someone that just stopped showing up to church and you never checked on them or even prayed for them. What about our pastors? Do we set them up on such unreasonably high pedestals, that it is just a matter of time before they fall? How much support do we offer, how much help do we give? Do we have huge expectations and then refuse to give the support for them to accomplish all the things we want? How do our expectations drive others into the ground? Do we force people into hypocrisy just to cover the fact that they can't meet our expectations!

The problem with the veil of hypocrisy is that it has no substance. You can see right through it. It is a smoke screen, a distraction, a magic trick.

Jesus warned, "Beware the leaven of the Pharisees, which is hypocrisy. Nothing is covered up that will not be revealed, or hidden that will not be known. Therefore, whatever you have said in the dark shall be heard in the light, and what you have whispered in private rooms shall be proclaimed on the housetops." (Luke 12:1-3)

Some people and some churches are very good at it. If you throw on enough screens, enough distractions, enough illusions, you can hide the truth. But eventually it fails. It is only through being open, honest, genuine and sincere in our love for Jesus

Christ, can we then allow everyone to see us for who we are; broken, sinful, fallen. So we can be seen as God sees us, as sinners, as lost sheep who are eager to find our Shepard.

We are called to simply love the Lord with all our hearts, with all our soul, and with all our minds, and to love our neighbors as we would love ourselves, to love, as we want to be loved. (Mat 22:34-40) It's time to drop the veil. You're not fooling anyone, and certainly not God. The church needs to be a place where we all can come and fall on our face and say, "I am not worthy, I have sinned and I have struggles", and for us as individuals and as the church to respond, "Oh yeah . . . me too! But let me help you up, because thanks be to God, Jesus suffered my stripes, took my beating, and hung on my cross, and He rose again, so that I can stand here today, in God's grace, in the love of Jesus Christ and the Holy Spirit, admit my sins and profess, it's ok!"

I WAS THINKING . . .

Am I quick to judge someone as a hypocrite before "walking a mile in their shoes"; before learning what's going on behind the behavior?

Do I get so consumed with my own problems, my own situation and quite frankly . . . me; that my behavior says to others—hypocrite?

Am I more likely to love someone or judge someone?

LOVE VS. JUDGMENT

It is an amazing feeling when we first get inspired to share the Gospel of Jesus Christ. Our hearts become lit on fire as we burn with a desire to share the joy and the love that we now experience in our salvation and in our new or renewed relationship with our Heavenly Father, His Son and His Spirit. It is a tremendous gift to feel a love for our fellow human beings and earnestly desire to give them every opportunity to be saved from eternal damnation. But what a slippery slope that is.

We become so passionate, we get excited and we become so in tuned to the prompting and the convictions of the Holy Spirit that we just want to share! And before we are even aware of it, we are telling the whole world what they are doing wrong. (What did he just say?)

We are called to love; the great commission is to love. Paul writes that, "faith, hope, and love abide, these three; but the greatest of these is love." (1st Corinthians 13:13). Paul also writes in Romans the 14th chapter; he warns against judging our neighbors and our fellow Christians and strongly cautions us against passing judgment.

Romans 14:1 "As for the one who is weak in faith, welcome him, but not to quarrel over opinions."

Romans 14:4-5; "Who are you to pass judgment on the servant of another? It is before his own master that he stands or falls. And he will be upheld, for the Lord is able to make him stand.

Romans 14:10-13; "Why do you pass judgment on your brother? Or you, why do you despise your brother? For we will all stand before the judgment seat of God; for it is written, "As I live, says the Lord, every knee shall bow to me, and every tongue shall confess to God." So then each of us will give an account of himself to God. Therefore, let us not pass judgment on one another any longer, but rather decide never to put a stumbling block or hindrance in the way of a brother."

So I suggest to you, when confronted with a brother that may not believe as we do or behave as we do; whether in the body of Christ or not, that we first try to love. We don't judge, condemn, convict or correct. Judgment we leave to God the Father through his son Jesus Christ. Conviction we leave to the helper of the Holy Spirit. And there is plenty of guilt and condemnation coming from the world, hell and the devil. What we need to do is L.O.V.E . . . first love them!

Pray before you think, think before you act, and let your actions always reflect your love.

I WAS THINKING . . .

I asked myself this question in the last thought, but it is an important question. Am I more likely to love someone or judge someone?

Do my actions towards others, especially those that don't share my beliefs reflect my love, or my judgment?

The bible, referring to followers of Christ, states that we will be recognized by our love . . . am I?

By this all people will know that you are my disciples, if you have love for one another." (John 13:35 ESV)

By this we know love, that he laid down his life for us, and we ought to lay down our lives for the brothers. (1 John 3:16 ESV)

Everyone who believes that Jesus is the Christ has been born of God, and everyone who loves the Father loves whoever has been born of him. By this we know that we love the children of God, when we love God and obey his commandments. (1 John 5:1-2 ESV)

LOVE YOUR ENEMY

CONFRONTING SOCIETY AS A CHRISTIAN

There are so many issues that we face in the world today that I *know* have the heart of God just breaking to see what we have become. As Christians, our hearts should also weep knowing the suffering that is in this world, and we should be even more saddened to look around and see so many that don't know the love of Jesus Christ; so many that may spend eternity separated from their Father in Heaven.

I have come to realize that I differ from some Christians on how these issues should be, and need to be addressed. Abortions, the homosexual movement, atheist and agnostics, spread of Islam as well as a variety of other social issues that Christians are faced with every day. These are all issues that so many are ready to stand against, to fight against. But what is our role?

Christians should want to ban together, to increase in numbers and be ready to combat all that interfere with the expansion of the Kingdom of Heaven. However; all these issues are no more than symptoms of a simpler, yet overwhelming

The problems facing the world today are not from a social sickness, it's from a heart sickness.

problem. All these issues that face society and Christians today are all issues of the heart; and because they are issues of the heart, they cannot be changed without changing the heart. An alcoholic will not change until he acknowledges there is a problem; an abuser will not change until he sees what he is doing to be so wrong and destructive. All who stand in opposition to God's laws, also stand in opposition to God's love.

Think about it; do you really think that anyone who would kill their baby, does it not thinking it is the right thing to do? Do you really believe that someone would live their life as a homosexual if they didn't believe in their heart what they were doing was ok? Do you really think that those who want to remove God from government, from society and from our schools don't believe in their heart of hearts that they are doing the right thing? All these people believe firmly in their hearts that they are right. Do you think that simply telling all these people that they are wrong is going to change their minds or change their hearts?

I have been struggling with watching the radical Islamic agenda as they spread their beliefs and their influence across the globe. The schools, the community, the society, the world at large seem to be encroaching on our beliefs, our freedoms . . . our rights.

As the homosexual community strives for more rights, more freedom, more acceptance; there is a push to change the laws to fit their goal. However, as "Christians" push back to "protect the sanctity of marriage" there becomes a head on collision of ideologies. How can we call ourselves a free country if we only allow people to express *their* freedom the way *we* think it should be expressed? (There are people picking their jaws off the floor at how much I sounded like a liberal there.)

> *We need to be less concerned about today and tomorrow, and more concerned about eternity!*

But follow me through on this for a minute. What are we talking about here? Are we talking about individual rights, societal rights, are we talking about the rights of one group versus the rights of another? Do we want to break it down to—what's right verses what's wrong. Do we want to make it a "religious" debate and put what my Bible says against your spiritual foundation? Are we talking about my rights versus your rights? Or is it that what we should be talking about is salvation?

As I have been wrestling with the questions of how I confront these issues of liberalism, homosexuality, abortion, radical Islam and other social issues; I continually struggle with the question of what is my role in defending what I believe to be true and holy. The questions always come down to how! How do I face these ideals that truly insult the foundation of my belief system; and yet stay within my belief system? I keep coming back to a question that just *irritates* me; "What would Jesus do?"

This is where I began to really come to some interesting conclusions: When Jesus himself was challenged on the "Law", he simply responded by questioning their heart. Jesus never confronted the social issues of the day. He never discussed politics. As a matter of fact when confronted on the issue of taxes he simply responded to give to Caesar what is Caesar's. The only noted time he got visibly angry was at those who misused the temple or at his disciples when they couldn't stay awake to pray with him. If someone wants your coat, give him your shirt (paraphrasing Mark 5:40). What is the greatest commandment? Love your God with all your heart and love your neighbor as yourself.

I come back to what are we talking about. Jesus spoke in terms of eternity, not in terms of tomorrow. Again, what are we talking about, are we talking about the problems with the world today or are we talking about eternity. The great commission is not to go into the entire world and confront sin. The great commission is to go into the entire world and proclaim the Gospel. We don't need more sermon's that point out sin and shame people with the "Law", we need to first hear and be reminded of the Gospel, then second how to tell others the Gospel . . . the good news!

I think we are missing it if the questions we are asking is how do we stop or how do we change or how do we convert. If someone points out to you; "hey, they are homosexuals!" The only response should be; "So? Have they heard about Jesus?" That is the only concern, because in the scope of eternity nothing else matters. It is only our pride that wants us to change the world, fix the world or keep the world from changing.

So what are we to do? It really is not all that complicated. The bible lays out clearly how we are to combat the forces of evil, to fight all those that stand in opposition to God. We love them. (SAY WHAT!) We love them, and in doing so, show them the love of God and all that He has done through His son, Jesus Christ. "And you shall love the Lord your God with all your heart and with all your soul and with all your mind and with all your strength. The second is this, you should love your neighbor as yourself.

We can become so concerned about what's going on "out there" that we miss what's right in front of us.

There is no other commandment greater than these." (Mark 12:30-31) Paul writes; "if your enemy is hungry, feed him; if he is thirsty, give him something to drink; for by doing so you will heap burning coals on his head [spiritually speaking]. Do not be overcome by evil, but overcome evil with good." (Romans 12:20-21) Let me put it another way; you can catch more flies with honey than you can with vinegar.

Please don't misunderstand; I am not saying to just lie down and let the world have its way. Be strong and be firm. Be a wall; a brick wall never struck or hurt anyone, it just stands. If there are political issues, get out and vote on them. If you come across someone who is in opposition to God's love, love them; and through that love becomes relationships; and through relationships you can show God's love; and in God's love and through the awesome power of the Holy Spirit, the heart can be changed. Nehemiah didn't ask everyone to build the whole wall, just the wall in front of them. (Nehemiah—read it if you don't know it!)

No one can be bullied, intimidated, threatened, coerced, scared, beaten, dragged, forced or even brainwashed into accepting the love of Christ. And if that is what it takes, quite frankly, He doesn't want it. Love your enemy, pray for them. There is enough condemnation in the world; conviction is the job of the Holy Spirit; we are called to love. Leave the judgment and condemnation to the world; we are called to accept, to support, to guide and above all . . . . to love! "He that is without sin among you, let him first cast a stone" (John 8:7).

I WAS THINKING . . .

Do those that stand in opposition to what I believe see my anger, my frustration and my disgust; or do they see my love?

What do those who have chosen to live a life rejecting God see in me; the condemnation of the "religious" or the love of Christ?

What does combating evil look like in my life? Am I standing firm or am I lashing out?

STAND FIRM

There is no doubt that getting through life today is no walk in the park. For those of us who have chosen to accept our salvation through faith, the enemy has been ever strong and vigilant. I've written much about loving our neighbor. For so many Christians, that just doesn't seem to be enough. We get a burning desire to fight all that goes against what we know to be right and wrong. There are so many issues that face our society today; one might not know where to begin.

However, this is where I want to take a moment to just ask you to take some time to take a deep breath, think before you act and spend a lot of time in prayer. Seek out what God would have you do to further His kingdom. Be careful you don't act out of furthering your own agenda.

There are many times in the Old Testament when God called on His people to enter into war, to fight battles, to conquer, to destroy and to eliminate. But remember, when those who were chosen to enter into battle, they were called by God. They acted under the direction of God and were only victorious because it was God's will; God's plan. Those that went to battle as part of God's will; entered it in confidence that His will would prevail. They could stand firm on who He is. Those who entered the battlefield against God's will or did not act as He instructed were defeated.

In today's world, there is not much call for conquering territory or obtaining land needed for survival. The issues that face us as Christians today are of civil liberties, religious rights and freedoms, social issues, and probably most sensitive, moral issues facing our society. There are growing issues that smack right in the face of Christian values; Godly values. As society continues its progressive move away from God, it attempts to change the laws to adapt to their want of a lack of accountability. To this I say, get involved, know what is going on in the legislature, know who is running for office, and get behind those politicians that support your point of view.

However I urge you to recognize, this is not a personal attack, and this is not about you. This is about others defying God. This is about removing God from society. No one can remove *your* personal convictions; no one can take away *your* accountability. Don't get angry and certainly don't hate them. It is from an angry and bitter heart that causes one to rebel against a God that has so much love for them. Fear and anger is not the way to confront those that are already hurt and angry; for that is no more than dumping fuel on a burning fire. We confront them with love and stand firm in our convictions.

When the Israelite's were fleeing their captors in Egypt, Moses said to them; "Fear not, stand firm, and see the salvation of the Lord, which he will work for you today." (Exodus 14:13) When Paul finishes his 1st letter to the church in Corinth, he tells them; "Be watchful, stand firm in the faith, act like men, be strong. Let all that you do be done in love." (1 Corinthians 16:13-14) Paul writes again to the church in Ephesus, instructing them on preparing their spiritual armor; "Therefore take up the whole armor of God, that you may be able to withstand in the evil day, and having done all, to stand firm." (Ephesians 6:13) Paul wrote to the church in Philippi from his imprisonment in Rome; imprisoned for simply spreading the Gospel of Jesus

Christ. Even while undergoing his own torment, he still wrote and instructed the church; "Only let your manner of life be worthy of the gospel of Christ, so that whether I come and see you or am absent, I may hear of you that you are ***standing firm*** in one spirit, with one mind striving side by side for the faith of the gospel, and not frightened in anything by your opponents." (Philippians 1:27-28)

We live in a time where we have more freedoms and liberties than any other time in history, yet we fear. Only one of the 12 disciples died of natural causes, all killed for their beliefs, for their faith and for spreading the good news of Jesus Christ; yet we live in fear and want to act out against those that challenge what we believe. Christ walked among us as an example of love and not of judgment, anger or fear. The bible that was written as a result of Christ; speaks of love and compassion. I urge you to seek to spread the Gospel, the good news of Jesus Christ; and I urge you to do so in love. For that is what we are called to do.

> "Preach the Gospel wherever you go, use words if necessary."
> -St Francis

I leave you with words from Paul's last letter to his spiritual son Timothy as he awaited his execution in Rome:

"I charge you in the presence of God and of Christ Jesus, who is to judge the living and the dead, and by his appearing and his kingdom: preach the word; be ready in season and out of season; reprove, rebuke, and exhort, with complete patience and teaching. For the time is coming when people will not endure sound teaching, but having itching ears they will accumulate for themselves teachers to suit their own passions, and will turn away from listening to the truth and wander off into myths. As for you, always be sober-minded, endure suffering, do the work of an evangelist, fulfill your ministry." (2 Timothy 4:1-5)

I WAS THINKING . . .

How many times in my life do I strike out, act out or move; all out of fear or uncertainty when God is telling me to stand still?

When I act, do I act out of patience or fear?

When chaos in my life occurs, do I turn to me or to prayer?

So many times in my life I could describe myself like a hamster in a wheel. Running my little butt off, but not going anywhere. It's when I stop, that things really take off!

HOW DO I DEAL WITH CONFLICT

I have noticed that in and around my life, dealing with conflict has been consuming more and more of my time and effort. I have noticed that most of the people I know have also been dealing with increased conflict in their lives as well. With more than 20 years of dealing with conflict in law enforcement and as an Emergency Room nurse, I would like to share just a couple of thoughts that have become staples in my philosophy with addressing conflict resolutions.

First, I want to speak on a spiritual level. When confronted with a situation of conflict, or when we are about to knowingly enter into a tense situation; we need to be in prayer, stay in prayer, and finish in prayer. Paul wrote in Ephesians chapter 6; "For we do not wrestle against flesh and blood, but against the rulers, against the authorities, against the cosmic powers over this present darkness, against the spiritual forces of evil in the heavenly places." (Ephesians 6:12) We have to understand and recognize that there is a spiritual battle that is going on around us. We need to engage in prayer so that we can call into play God our father, His son Jesus Christ, His Spirit and all the Angels in heaven to be involved in this spiritual battle; for we have no power or no authority in this realm. We need to turn it over to God and pray for His intervention.

Conflicts are never resolved in the presence of pride or emotion.

Next, I want to speak to three items of importance when dealing with our flesh and conflict. First, we need to remove our emotions from the situation. We have to remember that when dealing with conflict, it is not personal. Most conflict is born of lack of information, misinformation, miscommunication, anxiety, stress, and/or fear. The confrontation or conflict then is a result of someone acting out in response to their emotions. I urge you; do not enter onto the battlefield of emotional conflict; no one wins. Both parties get angry and both parties get hurt; no one wins. I urge you to check your emotions at the door; that leaves you better equipped to discern the source of the conflict which moves you quicker towards a resolution.

Second, stay calm. When we are confronted, our natural fight or flight mechanisms begin to kick into gear. Our adrenalin begins to pump; our heart rate increase and we begin to breath faster; we develop tunnel vision as our brain transitions from cognitive mode to reflexive mode; this is all as our body prepares to enter into physical battle or the run to safety. I urge you; when you feel this begin to happen, physically make yourself calm down, slow and deepen your breathing. Remove yourself from the situation for a time if necessary. The writer of Psalms 46 reminds us that; "God is our refuge and strength, a very present help in trouble." "Be still, and know that I am God." (Psalms 46:1, 10) Calm down, be still and know that it is in God's hands. Engage your brain and do not react out of a reflexive response to the situation.

Third, be patient. In our excitement to address or fix a problem, we can become very impatient and excited; then we act in hast when it may not be needed. Sometimes, when exercising a little patience, a situation will resolve itself or God will reveal His solution to the situation. I have been in a study and focus on Paul's second letter to Timothy. In the 4th chapter, Paul is advising Timothy; "preach the word; be ready in season and out of season; reprove, rebuke and exhort, with **complete patience** and teaching." (2 Timothy 4:2)

Conflict can be a very aggravating, stressful, burden that becomes increasingly heavy. However, if approached with the right outlook and attitude, conflict can be handled with peace and ease.

For those who work in the Law Enforcement or Security fields; even when physical confrontation is necessary to resolve a conflict; a calm controlled response is much more effective than a reflexive, emotional, chaotic response.

Remember to pray, remove your emotions, stay calm, and be patient and you will find that you will more quickly identify the source of the conflict and move faster towards resolving the conflict before it becomes a burden.

I WAS THINKING . . .

How many times have I entered into conflict as part of the problem instead of being part of the solution?

How many times have I allowed conflict to continue while knowing I was wrong?

How many times have I found myself in conflict as a result of my own mistakes or poor choices?

WHO KNOWS BEST

My pastor at church was talking about the Holy Spirit and he touched on a passage that at the time spoke to me, but the longer it sat on my heart, it has really began to move me. He was speaking from Romans 8:28, "And we know that all things work together for good to them that love God, to them who are the called according to His purpose". The point he was driving home is that God knows what is best for me. On hearing this concept, it was not new. Of course God knows what's best for me. That was no problem. God knows what's best; all I have to do is just trust in God, right? No problem . . . piece of cake . . . just trust in God . . . trust. (That's when I hit the big wall.)

Have you ever completely trusted someone. Have you ever released all control of everything and turned it totally over to anyone else. Think of an amusement park and getting on a roller-coaster. We watch the ride, we see where it goes, we know what is going to happen, but we still get on the ride with a little fear and apprehension as they strap us in and we relinquish control. Is it so exhilarating because we give up some control? (By the way, I *hate* roller-coasters.)

Let me just say now that I have some major trust issues. Most of my life, I have felt that the only person that I could trust . . . was me. At one point, I had felt that everyone I have known had let me down. I have crawled into a shell of trusting only in

God the creator knows best; trusting in that is a whole other issue!

myself and then no one can let me down or hurt me. So to say, trust in God, I find myself stopping and realizing that in order to do that, I have to give up my trust in ME! I have to admit when that realization first hit me, I had a little panic attack!

"Trust in the LORD with all your heart, and lean not on your own understanding." Proverbs 3:5. Say it, read it, sounds simple, but is it? Trust in the LORD with ALL your heart. I challenge you as I have challenged myself. Trust in the LORD, it is beyond all our understanding, but in that trust, relinquish control, turn it over to him. So I ask; where do we put God in our lives? Is he our first thought when we wake in the morning? Does he consume our every thought through the day? He wants to.

We need to turn it over to the Lord, trust in him, hand him the reigns and let him lead. All we do on our own or in our own name, is wasted time, wasted breath and wasted energy. "Unless the Lord builds the house, those who build it labor in vain. Unless the Lord watches over the city, the watchman stays awake in vain. It is in vain that you rise up early and go late to rest, eating the bread of anxious toil; for he gives to his beloved sleep." (Psalm 127:1-2)

I WAS THINKING . . .

Do I struggle with the thought that my Heavenly Father, the one who created me, the one who orchestrated the universe knows what's best for me?

When I do come to the realization that He does know what is best for me; do I trust Him?

Do I have faith in my Heavenly Father over my life?

(Going for an aspirin . . . be right back.)

WHERE'S MY JOY?

In a study series that I was in, I was confronted with a question that has plagued me most of my life. The most amazing part of all of this is the Edison moment (light bulb going off) that I received. What an epiphany it was to come to the realization, the understanding, the identification and unveiling; answering the question of **where's my joy!** (I lament . . .)

The study series that I was in that led to this huge moment in my life was on the subjects of Faith and Hope. Believe it or not, in the study of these questions, it ultimately led me back to the question of why I, and so many Christians, seem to be so devoid of joy. Where is the joy of the Lord? Shouldn't Christians experience joy? Does the bible not promise joy? Or does it? So I began to read; and to read very carefully.

God's word does not promise joy!

Through much study, thought and debate, I have chosen to study the Word (Bible) using the English Standard Version (ESV). And in that version, the word "joy" appears in 171 verses. (Yes, I read them all). And in not one of those verses is "joy" promised.

Are you kidding me?! Imagine my surprise to find out that there is no promise of joy in the Bible. Who lied to me?! Somebody shoot me!

So once I had calmed down and really began to understand what I was reading; it became crystal clear that even though there is no promise of joy; joy is right there in front of us. Let me explain.

The circle and whirlwind of questions that led me here comes from my own internal struggle with anxiety; particularly my anxiety over the future. In various times and stages in my life, I have attempted to get involved, become active in, or serve in a church. I found that I would quickly become discouraged and impatient when I felt that things weren't progressing fast enough or to be quite honest; when things weren't going my way. Things work out, they don't work out, churches split, I get angry . . . what is going on . . . why are things happening the way they are . . . who is in control here . . . what is my purpose? The questions go on and on. It is easy to get so wrapped up in attempting to understand and explain or even fix, that we lose our focus. We become so engrossed and consumed in our problems that we develop tunnel vision or just become blinded in our struggles and in our trials.

Who, what, why, when, how? These are not bad questions, not by any means. But to what degree do they consume our lives? I hate to go all "glass half full" on you, but really. How much do we focus on the negative? Look at the media of today, we have become a people of pain and drama junkies. The news is a constant stream of well . . . bad news! We can't get enough. Who watches a car race just in hopes to see a crash? Really?! So I ask the question; where is our focus? Where is our joy?

Things can bring us joy, but there is only one joy that is eternal!

So let's begin our study. If your focus is on things that are not of God and are of things of this world; your joy is temporary if not a complete deception all together. A new car might bring you a sense of joy, until you have to make the first payment. Spend and buy, mountains of debt; pleasures of the flesh, lifetime {or eternity} of regret. Have we become such a society of introspection and self-service? Has our vision become so short sighted that more and more of our daily thoughts are consumed with making us feel good? Is the growing epidemic of addiction in this country and around the world more about our desire for instant gratification? Where is our focus? What are we trying to satisfy: is it our needs or our lusts, is it our needs or our desires, do we want true joy or just a quick fix? (There are a couple commandments that warn us about coveting.) Where is our focus!?

In a search for answers to these questions, I turned to God's Word, to the bible. Again; 171 verses that contain the word "joy"; here are just a few:

> You (LORD) make known to me the path of life; in your presence there is **fullness of joy**; at your right hand are pleasures forevermore. (Psalms 16:11)

> Many are the sorrows of the wicked, but steadfast love surrounds the one who trusts in the Lord. Be glad in the Lord, and rejoice, O righteous, and **shout for joy**, all you upright in heart! (Psalms 32:10-11)

> The **hope of the righteous brings joy**, but the expectations of the wicked will perish. (Proverbs 10:28)

> Though the fig tree should not blossom, nor fruit be on the vines, the produce of the olive fail and the fields yield no food, the flock be cut off from the fold and there be no herd in the stalls, yet I will rejoice in the LORD; **I will take joy in the God of my salvation**. (Habakkuk 3:17-18)

Jesus said; "I am the true vine, and my father is the vinedresser. Every branch in me that does not bear fruit he takes away, and every branch that does bear fruit he prunes, that it may bear more fruit. Already you are clean because of the word that I have spoken to you. Abide in me, and I in you. As the branch cannot bear fruit by itself, unless it abides in the vine, neither can you unless you abide in me. I am the vine; you are the branches. Whoever abides in me and I in him, he it is that bears much fruit, for apart from me you can do nothing. If anyone does not abide in me he is thrown away like a branch and withers; and the branches are gathered, thrown into the fire, and burned. If you abide in me, and my words abide in you, ask whatever you wish, and it will be done for you. By this my Father is glorified, that you bear much fruit and so prove to be my disciples. As the Father has loved me, so have I loved you. Abide in my love. If you keep my commandments, you will abide in my love, just as I have kept my Father's commandments and abide in His love. **These things I have spoken to you, that my joy may be in you, and that your joy may be full**. John 15:1-11

We are not promised joy; we are given promises of where our joy lies or can be found. Our joy resides in His presence; our joy is found in Him! Sure, things happen in this life that can bring us joy, but those things of this world are short lived. I can express my joy in my children, but my joy cannot depend on my children. Children get hurt, they get sick, they rebel, they become teenagers, they get angry, and they eventually leave to live their own lives (hopefully in Christ). Things can bring us joy, but there is only one joy that is eternal!

> *Pain is* **necessary** *for growth.*

Then why is there so much pain? What a good question, but again I am going to defer to our primary question; where is our focus? When we focus on the pain of our circumstances, we are unable to see the value in the lesson. When I was at Paris Island (Marine Corps Boot Camp), my only focus was to get through as fast as I could, not realizing the benefits of the physical, psychological, and emotional training I was receiving for combat and well, for life. Pain promotes growth. Look at it solely on a physical level. Here are some physical training mottos: no pain, no gain; pain is weakness leaving the body; and so on. Pain is necessary for physical growth, for physical improvement. The same principles apply to emotional growth. It is only through emotional trials that we are able to obtain emotional growth. Knowledge comes from learning, from studying, from painful effort. Wisdom comes from experiences, some from good, but most from bad!

Count it all joy, my brothers, when you meet trials of various kinds, for you know that the testing of your faith produces steadfastness. (James 1:2-3)

I will be the first to admit, there are a lot of pains that I do not understand. But if I can keep my trust in God, maintain my faith in Him, keep my Hope in His promises; maybe I can get through the pain, learn His lesson, to see His glory!

I leave you with these final thoughts. Spend time in the Bible, for it is the written thoughts and commandments of God. Where is your focus; is you focus on God's word?

> Your words were found, and I ate them, and **your words became to me a joy** and the delight of my heart, for I am called by your name, O LORD, God of hosts. (Jeremiah 15:16)

What is your focus; do your actions reflect your focus?

> But I say, walk by the Spirit, and you will not gratify the desires of the flesh. For the desires of the

flesh are against the Spirit, and the desires of the Spirit are against the flesh, for these are opposed to each other, to keep you from doing the things you want to do. But if you are led by the Spirit, you are not under the law. Now the works of the flesh are evident: sexual immorality, impurity, sensuality, idolatry, sorcery, enmity, strife, jealousy, fits of anger, rivalries, dissensions, divisions, envy, drunkenness, orgies, and things like these. I warn you, as I warned you before, that those who do such things will not inherit the kingdom of God. But the **fruit of the Spirit** is love, **joy**, peace, patience, kindness, goodness, faithfulness, gentleness, self-control; against such things there is no law. And those who belong to Christ Jesus have crucified the flesh with its passions and desires.

If we live by the Spirit, let us also keep in step with the Spirit. (Galatians 5:16-25 ESV)

If we keep our focus on Him and in Him, there too will we find our joy!

I WAS THINKING . . .

Where do I look to find my joy; in things of this world or in things of eternal value found in my Heavenly Father?

Does someone steal my joy or do I give it away?

When I find myself without joy, what am I focusing on?

CELEBRATE THE VICTORIES

I was tasked with helping a friend through a difficult time in his life. He had lost a couple family members in recent years and his pain was capped with the loss of his father. I began to ponder what it was I could say to him to help him through this horrific time in his life. It was quickly apparent to me that there was nothing I could say to in any way ease his pain.

I soon began to dwell on how I, how we as humans, we as Christians, deal with our pain and an image began to unfold in my head. Most of us have seen the movie "Brave Heart". Mel Gibson played a character based on the real life story of William Wallace who led Scotland in a revolt against England. Anyway, the scene that came to mind was one of the big battle scenes of the movie. Each side starts on one or the other side of an open field, a charge is given and they meet in the middle for what amounts to hand to hand combat. It's a gruesome scene that is quite graphic (definitely a guy scene in a guy movie). But what is really sticking in my mind is the first images immediately after the battle. The camera goes to William Wallace, standing in the middle of this field, covered in blood and bodies lying all around him just covering the field. He and others that fought with him then give out this loud yell. A scream, a cry . . . . a victory shout!

> *We must acknowledge that life is a physical, emotional and spiritual battle!*

69

They knew the battle was coming. For days anxiety and fear had to be mounting up inside of them. The anticipation and anxiety prior to the battle had to be overwhelming. The battle itself was for your life, kill or be killed; the physical and emotional demands had to be exhausting beyond description. And when finished, the first thing done . . . is a shout of victory! What a display, what a vision!

You cannot watch a single sporting event even to this day that when an event is won, hands go in the air and a shout is made. There is a celebration. A physical and emotional display of a hard battle fought and won. Now don't get me wrong, soon after there is a debriefing, a reflection, a review and maybe even a time of mourning. We watch the tapes. What we did right, what did we do wrong, how can we get better. But before all this is a celebration. Even in battles, war, in combat, and in "Brave Heart". There was time to reflect, to lament, to mourn the loss and bury the dead. But before all that was the celebration of a hard fought victory.

I have noticed that we as Christians spend a lot of time in reflection, hung up on all that we have been through and may have to go through. There is not a Christian alive who doesn't reference the book of Job in reflecting on their own life. And rightfully we should. Our journey is a challenge. In the letters of the New Testament, Paul often spoke of our journey not as a walk, but as a marathon. We are here on Earth, stuck between Heaven and Hell, not just in the physical, but in the spiritual. Our journey is not easy . . . and is not meant to be. We should daily take time to acknowledge that we are in a battle and prepare ourselves accordingly. In Ephesians, Paul speaks of the "armor of God", and how we should invest time in taking care of and making sure that our armor is battle ready.

What I have come to realize is that I, that we as Christians, as followers of Jesus Christ, what we often forget to do, is celebrate the victories. It's Sunday morning, it's been a long week, just one day to sleep in, yet you get out of bed and make it to church, CELEBRATE THE VICTORY! You're a young teenager, friends pressuring you to go partying, do drugs, drink, you say no. Don't pout over what you may have missed, CELEBRATE THE VICTORY! Your church has just split, friends and family divided, feeling hurt, bodies lying all over from the battle, but you survive and with your faith intact, CELEBRATE THE VICTORY! My friend has struggled to care for his father as he slowly deteriorated and eventually passed. The road was long and hard, few could have survived the battle, but days after his father passed, he gave his life to Christ. He survived the battle! And yes, time should be given to reflect, to mourn and to take account, but let's not forget to take time to celebrate our victories.

I WAS THINKING . . .

I never forget to pout when things aren't going well, but do I spend any time celebrating when things do go well?

In my everyday conversations, do I spend more time griping about how bad things are or do I talk about the good things, the blessings in my life?

I have no problem calling on someone to help me whine or throw a "pity party"; how often do I share all the daily (and maybe minor) victories in my life?

Do I celebrate the victories in my life?!

SOME *REALLY* HEAVY THOUGHTS!

ACKNOWLEDGED MAN

I just want to share with you a quick summary of what it has meant to me to becoming an acknowledged man, as I share some thoughts that I am just now beginning to understand.

Let's start with a definition—acknowledge: Dictionary.com defines as to admit to be real or true; recognize the existence, truth, or fact of. Merriam says to recognize the rights, authority, or status of. So before I go one step further; I want us to have an understanding of what it means to acknowledge something; to recognize the truth or fact, the authority, the *"right"*. I have discovered that in my search to discover what it was to be a Godly father, a Godly husband, a Godly man; there were several things that I had to first acknowledge.

This is not an end all to the secrets of life. This will not solve all your problems. But if you will acknowledge some simple truths; it can be the foundation of what you build the rest of your life on. I discussed three things a second ago; being a Godly father, a Godly husband, and a Godly man. One of the things that tie these all together is relationships; relationship with your children, relationship with your wife and relationship with your Heavenly Father. I believe that if you acknowledge the next seven truths, you will have a foundation on which to build your future as a Godly man.

Acknowledge your anger.

It has taken me nearly 20 years of parenting along with 20 years of marriage to get this one. You have to acknowledge your anger. Anger is an emotion that will wreak havoc on every aspect of your life. Anger is born out of our frustrations, our disappointments, our fears . . . our anxieties. Most times it is our inability to identify and then resolve the things that frustrate and irritate us that will ultimately anger us. We have to be willing and able to acknowledge the anger inside of us. It is then, and only then that we can begin to address the issues, deal with them appropriately and move past them.

Understand it is ok to get angry; until we bury it, deny it, ignore it or suppress it. Anger is the primary instrument that drives wedges, builds walls and destroys relationships and it needs to be acknowledged so it can be addressed. In acknowledging your anger, you need to understand that you cannot get full and true healing from your anger without the help of your Heavenly Father. You need to give it to God. You need to turn it over to Jesus Christ.

Acknowledge you need help.

As human beings, we are born with an innate sense of our own superiority. We, some worse than others, have our own delusions of grandeur and feel that we can take care of things ourselves. We need help. We need help from friends, advisors, spiritual leaders. In some cases we may even need to seek help from professionals. But in all circumstances, we need help from our Heavenly Father. Seek earnestly in prayer and His Word for guidance and solutions to the struggles and problems we encounter. Acknowledge your limitations and seek help!

Acknowledge your faults.

You want me to do WHAT! Isn't it amazing that we all can spend a lifetime pointing out the faults in others. We can pick just about everyone we know apart. Making a list of others shortcomings is as easy as passing gas. Where we fall short is seeing the problems in ourselves. If we want to see real change in our lives, real change in our relationships; it begins with us. The first step to change is admitting you need to change. The hardest part and the most important part, is admitting we are part of the problem. (Man this guy hits below the belt.)

Acknowledge what you cannot control.

Thoughts are spinning through your head. You are searching for something better. You want to be the best father and husband you can be. You keep thinking; "But **_they_** are just being so difficult!" You need to acknowledge you have absolutely no control over *their* behavior, *their* actions, or *their* feelings. So stop trying to change them; you can't. Stop trying to control them; you can't. So now it's on you. Now for some more good news, you really don't have the power to change you either. (What?!) On your own will you can make temporary adjustments to your behavior, but it will not last. The anger and the frustration will creep back in. If you truly want to be a better husband and father. You need to ask and allow your Heavenly Father through the Holy Spirit to change your heart. You can try other ways, you can try it on your own, but if you want true change; you need Christ. Ask Jesus to change your heart; **then** allow Him to change your heart. As your heart changes, so will your behavior. As your behavior changes, you will see those around you begin to change. As you pray for them, God will begin to work on their heart as well. (As a note, don't expect anything overnight, don't expect anything at all! Just know He is working.) So acknowledge what you can control. You control your will; you control your decisions. Outside of that, you control nothing. You cannot control those around you. You cannot control your circumstance or your environment. You cannot control the world around you. And you certainly cannot control God. Acknowledge it. Then surrender it; let it go! Control is an illusion and the more you buy into the illusion, the more frustrated, and angry you will grow. LET IT GO!

Acknowledge your position.

I was at a marriage conference once with my wife. On the third day of the conference we were divided by gender and the speaker said something that hit me like a sledge hammer on jello. He said that as men, we like the verse in the bible that speaks to man being "head of the household". He went on to explain that on the Day of Judgment, when we stand before God, it's our head. (WHAT!?) We will be held accountable not only for ourselves, but our wives, our children and our household. That thought scared the "cocky" right out of me! As head of the household, I will be held accountable not only for myself, but for my family.

Now I'm not saying we will be held accountable for their decisions and their mistakes, but we will be held accountable for what and how we affected their lives and their decisions. We have been placed at the head; we have been placed in charge; we have been made accountable; we are responsible. Now if you think that makes you dictator of your household, good luck with that. Love your household as Christ loved the church. You really need to search out and understand what it means to be a Godly leader. What it means to set the example, to love, to guide, to love, to teach, to love, to forgive, to love, to honor, to love, to mentor, to love, to shepherd, to love, to pastor, to love, to show Christ, to love . . . to lead.

Acknowledge your responsibility.

Whether you like it or not, you have responsibilities as a man. If you have chosen the life of a husband and/or father; your responsibilities have greatly multiplied. As a man, you are responsible for your actions. As a husband and father, you are responsible for your wife and for your family. They are ***your*** responsibility. To provide for, to protect, to encourage, to love, to lead, to guide, to honor, to teach, to submit to, to sacrifice for, to humble to, to be strong for, to cry with, to hold on to . . . their every need is ***your*** responsibility. God has entrusted them to YOU! Like it or not, it is the role you have chosen. I have to admit, a lot of days it is a role I would gladly surrender. But it's not the job of my parents, her parents, friends, church or the government . . . It's MY responsibility! (Even writing this causes an ache deep inside me . . .)

Acknowledge God.

If you are attempting any of this without acknowledging who God is, how He works, what Jesus Christ did for you . . . you are truly lost. You have to acknowledge that God through the Holy Spirit, who has made Himself available through the sacrifice of Jesus Christ; wants to be a part of every aspect, of every challenge, of every victory, of every minute of your life. Invite Him in, let Him in! Because there is one final truth that is present whether you acknowledge it or not; the devil will always be there and he will not stop in his attempt to derail, destroy, frustrate you, attack you, and anger you; all in hopes that you will turn your anger on your family and then on God. Satan will not stop, so you might as well seek the only one who has defeated him! Paul wrote to be "praying at all times"; never ceasing, never tiring or wavering, never doubting, never surrendering. I have to constantly remind myself in the times I have; ceased, tired, wavered, doubted and even surrendered. But in all my weaknesses . . . it was then that he "carried me"!

This again is not the end all, it is only the beginning. These are simple truths that have taken me more than two decades to get; and they seem to be common factors in the struggles for all of us. Most men I have known have already acknowledged these truths or they are stuck. If you are among the stuck; I hope that you will take advantage of my twenty years of struggle and meditate on these truths; acknowledge these truths! Step up to an understanding of what it is to be a Godly father, a Godly husband . . . a Godly man!

I pray that your Heavenly Father guides you, directs you and comforts you as you continue on this journey with me to being an acknowledged man. Together in Christ; may He grant us His wisdom, His serenity and His peace!

I WAS THINKING . . .

The hardest part of being an honest person is willing to be honest with myself. Am I truly willing to be honest with myself?

Am I strong enough to admit my shortcomings and take the steps necessary to correcting them?

What exists in my life, that I am not willing to acknowledge, but is holding me back from the man I have been called to be?

Have I chosen a life of blame or accountability?

PRAYER

I write this to be a very short reference on prayer. It is not in any means meant to be comprehensive; but just a brief reference guide to help get you started, or for you to use to help get someone else started. I want to strongly emphasize that prayer is simply talking to God; there is no format or required guidelines. Just talk to Him!

So what is prayer? Prayer is personal communication with God. Prayer includes; request for ourselves or others (intercession or petitions), confession of sin, adoration, praise and thanksgiving, and also God communicating to us indications of his response.

Why does God want us to pray? Prayer is an expression of faith, an acknowledgement of His existence, an expression of trust. Prayer is communication which is the foundation of a relationship. God wants us to love him, trust him, and have fellowship with him. Our fellowship is in our prayer; our investment in the relationship is through our prayer.

Why do we ask?
You do not have, because you do not ask (James 4:2)
Ask and it will be given to you; seek, and you will find; knock, and it will be opened to you. For everyone who asks receives, and he who seeks finds, and to him who knocks it will be opened. (Luke 11:9-10)
Asking is an acknowledgment of our need and our reliance on our Heavenly Father.

References in Matthew
How to pray; Mat 6:5-15
Reassurance; Mat 7:7-11, 21:22 (ask and it will be given)
Story of faith; Mat 8:5-13 (centurion's servant)
Parable of Sower; Mat 13:1-9, 18-23
Prayer changes God; Mat 15:21-28 (faith of Canaanite woman)
Jesus Prays; Mat 26:36-46

Additional thought on prayer . . .

There is a phrase that I have used on so many occasions and I have heard so many people, especially Christian's use. Finally one day it just smacked me so hard that the dog looked at me like; "what just happened?" I was listening to a close friend of mine telling me a story about a child she knew that was going through a tremendous amount of suffering. Her heart was breaking at the amount of pain in this child's life and there was nothing she could do. Out of desperation, she resolved to a last ditch effort; "I guess all I can do is just pray."

Now, I don't know why after all my life that phrase hit me so hard, but it did. Why is it, that when we refer to asking for intervention from the creator of the universe, we give it the same amount of weight as when discussing financial struggles we say; "well, maybe I'll win the lottery"? Do we really believe that an answered prayer has the same odds as the lottery? Is it a; "well if all else fails . . . here's hoping" kind of approach to prayer.

The truth of the matter is . . . no matter what is going on in our lives, no matter the situation, the drama or the dilemma; the only thing we *need* to do . . . is pray! Now here goes the lazy Christian who says; "I don't have to do anything, God will provide." To those I say yes, God will provide the harvest, if you sew and prepare the field. (I just offended somebody.)

The point that I am trying to make, the heart of what I am trying to get you to understand is that our Heavenly Father not only wants to be in on the conversation, He wants to be part of the solution, if you will call on Him. Not as an afterthought or a cliché; but as an active and sometimes only solution needed. The Holy Bible promises that God hears the prayers of the righteous.

I think our dilemma lies in not getting the answer we want or in the time we wanted it, so we assume our prayers go unanswered. In our "I want it now" and "I want it my way" world; we don't even take the time to recognize when God does answer our prayers and intervenes in our lives.

We need to have the mindset that in all aspects of our lives, we need to start in prayer, stay in prayer and finish in prayer and thanksgiving. I believe in all my heart of hearts that God will honor our every prayer that comes from a right heart and truly seeks for God's heart and His glory.

Let me leave you with some thoughts:

> Rejoice in hope, be patient in tribulation, be constant in prayer. (Romans 12:12 ESV)

> "praying at all times in the Spirit, with all prayer and supplication" (Ephesians 6:18 ESV)

> The Lord is at hand; do not be anxious about anything, but in everything by prayer and supplication with thanksgiving let your requests be made known to God. (Philippians 4:5-6 ESV)

> Continue steadfastly in prayer, being watchful in it with thanksgiving. (Colossians 4:2 ESV)

> The LORD has heard my plea; the LORD accepts my prayer. (Psalm 6:9 ESV)

> But truly God has listened; he has attended to the voice of my prayer. Blessed be God, because he has not rejected my prayer or removed his steadfast love from me! (Psalm 66:19-20 ESV)

But you still find yourself asking the question; "is God really answering or even hearing my prayers?" What you are really saying is that you are lacking faith and confidence. There are 2 steps to resolving these issues:

One is endurance. You have to pray, pray some more and keep praying. I love those that say; "I tried to exercise for a week, but I didn't see any results so I quit." Prayer is no different. If you want to build faith and confidence, you have to exercise your prayer and stay with it. If you don't use it, you'll lose it. (That applies to so much, doesn't it?!)

The second is to record. If you want to "see" how much God is doing in your life; keep a journal. I want you to start a daily journal of your prayers. After several months, look back over your journal and marvel at all God has done and is doing in your life! To get really blown away, do it for a year or two. I dare you!!

> Rejoice always, pray without ceasing, give thanks in all circumstances; for this is the will of God in Christ Jesus for you. (1 Thessalonians 5:16)

> Pray for all people. (1 Timothy 2)

> The prayer of faith. (James 5:13-18)

I WAS THINKING . . .

How often do I pray?

How often does God want me to be in prayer?

How is my prayer time spent: in thanksgiving, in worship, in communion . . . or is it always a list of request?

Is my prayer about me, or about Him?

BIBLE: FACT OR FICTION

You know, I have to tell you. I have taken much pride in including scripture references in almost all of my writings. But for the first time, and only GOD knows if it will be the only time, I am going to write without the use of a single scripture reference. I just don't believe there is any reference to any scripture or religious writing that can help you with this topic. So let's begin.

Every new Christian or any person who has not yet given their life to Jesus Christ but has begun attending church, or exploring their personal religious or spiritual beliefs; comes to a place where they question the validity of the Bible. And if you are one of those who have found yourself in this place, do not think yourself a horrible person, know that everyone of us have or will ask the question, "Is the Bible true?"

Now to those that have or are currently asking that very question; there are a multitude of references that I can give you that point to the validity of the Bible. If you are interested, please e-mail me and I would be happy to send those references to you. However, after having many conversations with a great deal of people, I have come to realize that it doesn't matter. It doesn't matter what I say, it doesn't matter what references I give, it doesn't matter what I can prove. Eventually, every person has to face and make that decision of: Do I, or don't I believe the Bible is true?

If you are struggling with that question, let me make it a little harder for you. To make your decision more complex, let me tell you something that makes your decision a little more difficult. The real question you need to answer is; is the Bible fiction, or non-fiction. Is the Bible fiction, which means false and made up; or is the Bible non-fiction, which means that every book, every chapter, and every word is the written word of GOD? Written word of GOD, written down by the hand of man as inspired by the Holy Spirit as directed by GOD.

Now, fiction books can be based on actual events, set in places that actually exist, but the stories are made up; just quite simply not true. And I have to tell you, there are a lot of people that place the Bible in that category. Or there are those that have chosen to accept some parts of the Bible as being true and other parts as being made up. What you have done, intentionally or not, is just place the Bible in the category of fiction.

The first steps towards questioning GOD, is questioning His word!

Let me give you just a quick example of how dangerous it is to just believe in just parts of the Bible. Muslims believe in God referred to as "Allah". Muslims believe they are the descendants of, and followers of Abraham. Muslims believe in Jesus as a great profit, just not the son of GOD. They believe in Mary and the virgin birth; in fact there is more written in the Koran about Mary than in the Christian Bible. The very second you start picking and choosing what you do and don't want to believe about the Bible, you have just placed the Bible in the category of fiction and started down a very dangerous road of lies and deception. (Which I might add, is exactly where the devil wants to lead you.)

This is a foundational, fundamental challenge that all Christians, me included, have had to address, face and overcome. GOD exists, and the Bible is true! The air I breathe I cannot see, but every breath is a testimony to its existence. The universe around us is a testimony to the existence and power of GOD and to those who have chosen to crack the pages of the Bible and allowed it to change them is a testimony to its validity.

There is a Bible verse that continues to ring in my mind when I find those who don't believe the Bible or choose to only believe parts of the Bible. [Here comes the scripture reference. I knew I couldn't do it, so I lied . . . Write my pastor!] "For the time is coming when people will not endure sound teaching, but having itching ears they will accumulate for themselves teachers to suit their own passions, and will turn away for listening to the truth and wander off into myths." 2 Timothy 4:3-4

The Holy Bible is the truth. It is the written word of our Heavenly Father. Your decision to accept or reject it does not change its truth. Here is another fact that I have found to be very true. Most of those that I have talked to that most strongly challenge the validity of the bible have never read it!

So to those who want to challenge the validity of the Bible, I issue a challenge of my own. Before you come to me and want to question whether or not the Bible is true . . . read it. Not just a couple chapters or a few pages. Remember the Bible is not *a* book; it is a collection of books. Read the New Testament, read the Old Testament. Read it from front to back or just pick a book and go. There are a million references out there on "how to read the Bible in a year". *[I have to say that I get a giggle from the people that will read a 600 page "Harry Potter" book in a week, but need a year to read the Bible.]*

In addition, to those who have read and/or studied the Holy Bible and still question; or for heaven's sake will preach that parts of the Bible are "only stories". I don't want to discuss the validity of the bible; I want to discuss your relationship with its author. I must remind you that the written word of God, our Bible is there for 2 primary reasons. One: to provide a resource for you to grow in your knowledge, understanding and ultimately your relationship with your Heavenly Father. Secondly: to serve as a reference for you to share and teach others. If you are one who believes they have been saved by Jesus Christ and have been accepted into the Body of Christ and your eternal salvation is secured, but you question any part of the Bible. I strongly encourage you to re-evaluate your relationship and therefore your understanding of, and with your Heavenly Father.

May the GOD of the universe and the Lord of Lords, our Heavenly Father bless you and bring you to a place of relationship and better understanding of who He is and a better understanding of His written WORD!

I WAS THINKING...

Can I question the word of my spouse without harming the relationship? Hence, can I question any part of the bible (God's word) without harming the relationship?

When I question the bible, am I really questioning my own faith?

In a struggle to accept the bible as true, am I questioning its validity or its content? Is it that I don't believe it to be true, or I don't want it to be true?

SALVATION

I was once presented with a question about salvation. The question was along the lines of when and how God grants his salvation and can He take it back, or the heart of the question was can we lose it? The question in itself can be a very frightening one, but one that I think can be answered very easily.

First let us define the word "salvation"; the act of saving from harm, deliverance from sin through Jesus Christ (Encarta Dictionary). Next, let us define "grace"; the infinite love, mercy, favor, and goodwill shown to humankind by God, the condition of being free of sin (Encarta Dictionary). Finally, we also need to define "faith"; the belief in, devotion to, or trust in (Encarta Dictionary).

God the Father, in His "*infinite* love, mercy, and favor", has saved us from the penalty of sin; through the sacrifice, suffering, and death of Jesus Christ His Son; requiring nothing more than our belief, trust and devotion to.

"But GOD, being rich in mercy, because of the great love with which he loved us, even when we were dead in our trespasses (sin), made us alive together with Christ—by grace you have been saved—and raised us up with Him and seated us with Him in the heavenly places in Christ Jesus, so that in the coming ages, He might show the immeasurable riches of His grace in kindness toward us in Christ Jesus. For by grace you have been saved through faith. And this is not your own doing; it is the gift of GOD, not a result of works, so that no one may boast. For we are his workmanship, created in Christ Jesus for good works, which GOD prepared beforehand, that we should walk in them."—Ephesians 2:4-10

Our salvation is never in question; it is never, "not there". Through His gift, through Jesus Christ, salvation exists for everyone, for all time. The only requirement, the only act, the only condition or prerequisite is our "faith". All we have to do is believe, to accept, to trust; GOD says here it is, all you have to do is take it, and because of His infinite love that is many times beyond our understanding, he gives us the choice to accept it, or pass it by. He will **_never_** take it away; however (pause for effect . . .), we can by our own decision, choose to turn from it and reject it. So, can we lose it, the answer is emphatically NO. Can we choose to turn from it, unfortunately we can.

Now pay attention, once "saved" we *will* sin. And as long as we continue to seek forgiveness, God's grace has no boundaries. As well, if you choose to willfully disobey and offend Him, His judgment is equally certain!

Once in the body of Christ, once saved, once we have made the decision to accept our free gift of salvation from sin and death; it then becomes most important for us to stay in prayer, stay in the word, stay in our relationship with GOD and get in a family of fellow Christians, a family of support. Being "saved" is not a one-time prayer or a one-time ceremony . . . it is a daily decision; a daily decision to be accepted as this wonderful gift through faith.

Know this, Satan will stop at NOTHING to get us angry, frustrated and/or defeated using any method he can to get us to turn from GOD, to lose our faith, to turn from our salvation. But in GOD, through Jesus Christ, and by the power of the Holy Spirit, in a simple act of faith, a simple act of trust, Satan is defeated and we are saved!

I WAS THINKING . . .

Do I take my salvation for granted?

If I have made a decision to accept my salvation, do my actions reflect my decision?

If I do believe a price was paid for my salvation, do I show any appreciation for the sacrifice?

SALVATION CAUTIONS

It has been the topic of many discussions in the small circle of people that I come into contact with. It never fails that when you are discussing religion or theology and the subject of "salvation" comes up, there always seems to be a difference of opinions. I am not God, and the Bible clearly states that only Jesus will be the one to sit in judgment of us when our Earthly life has expired. But if I may, let me tell you a couple of stories that might help with or maybe even change your perspective:

There was a man in who grew up loving a professional football team. His father, brothers and his uncle's loved and followed the team. At a very young age, he quickly adopted the family tradition of loving their hometown team. He knew all there was to know about his favorite football team. He could recite to you every player and their number that had ever played. He was an encyclopedia of knowledge about the team's history and background. The man was sure to never miss a game. He could rattle off statistics on each current player, so much so that he could tell you the names of their families and where they lived. The man wore their jerseys, had jewelry displaying the team logo. Everywhere he went all he did was brag on and praise the team. There was no greater fan or promoter.

It had since neared the end of his life and at the age of 75 years old, he requested a meeting with the owner of the team. In that meeting he recanted all his knowledge of the team and its history. He spoke of how he had never missed a game and how faithful he had been. He told of how loyal he has stayed and how tirelessly he had been promoting the team. He told of all the paraphernalia that he owned and never left his house without wearing something that represented the team.

Finally, after listening to several minutes of this man's testimony, the owner stopped him and told him that he was flattered and appreciated the loyal support, but wanted to know what he could do for the man. The man paused only for a brief moment and said, "Sir, I have worked my whole life promoting and supporting this team. Now at the end of my life, I would like to be paid." The owner paused and with a puzzled look on his face responded, "Sir, I appreciate your support, but you don't work for me and I don't know you."

There was another man who met a woman and a short time after meeting, they decided to get married. It took no time to set up the wedding and the ceremony was very nice. They exchanged rings, he recited some vows out of a book and it was done.

Right after the wedding however, the man continued to live as if he was single. He came and went as he pleased, worked long hours at a job that required a lot of travel, had relationships with many women. He stayed out all the time and would only visit home about 4 times a month.

His wife was very patient and accepted the situation as it was; but after what seemed like a lifetime, she had enough and the man found himself standing in front of a judge. The man was stunned and pleaded with the judge, "But sir; I did the ceremony; I wear the ring; I pay my bills; I tell all I know that I'm married; I don't understand!" The judge simply looked at the man and asked; "Do you have a relationship with your wife?" The man stood in silence . . . . the divorce—final.

Our salvation is free and guaranteed. The price for our sins has been paid in full through the love of our Father and the sacrifice of His Son Jesus Christ. Our eternal salvation has been bought, paid for, and assured.

I would like to offer a word of caution. Do you believe that your eternal soul is resting on the fact that you were a good promoter, or you wear the jewelry? Do you believe that because you performed some ceremony or recited a prayer; the security of your eternal soul is locked in? Your Heavenly Father loves you. He has provided you every opportunity to enter His Kingdom. Search your heart and your soul. Do not find yourself standing in front of our Lord Jesus Christ on the day of judgment and hear him say; "But I don't know you."

If this describes you; I beg of you. Find a quiet place and get down on your knees and earnestly and honestly begin a relationship with your Heavenly Father. There is no magic prayer; there are no magic words or ceremonies. Just in your plain words, in your plain language . . . talk to Him. Get to know your Father, for He longs to know you!

Your Father is calling!

I WAS THINKING . . .

Am I certain where I am going to spend eternity?

Has my salvation been based on reciting a prayer or performing a ceremony?

Do I have a relationship with my Heavenly Father or am I just visiting about 4 times a month?

Am I in a ritual or a relationship?

BAPTISM

Writing on this topic was a long time coming. I have to be honest with you; just the subject of "baptism" had been on my mind for some time (talking years, people). I also enter into this topic full well knowing that there is a HUGE divide among Christians on what it means to be "baptized" and exactly what that process is supposed to look like.

What has made the topic so hot on my mind might require a little background. I was raised a very devout and strict Catholic. Without rambling on and muddying the waters, I parted from my Catholic background and searched out through the denominations of what I felt God was after; what I was after. I have found myself most comfortable in a "non-denominational" church. I have found that for me, by removing the denominations, you begin to remove *most* of the "religion". (I'm going to take a short break and let you chew on that for a minute . . . .).

However, our church (that is the church that I attend and have become a part of) was conducting a census and was asking those that attended to join in a "partnership" with the church and to fill out a form stating such. The form, however, had a couple small requirements.

One—have entered into a personal relationship with Jesus Christ. (OK, I'm not having any problem with this.) Two—have been baptized (or will be in the next 6 months) as a follower of Christ as a public declaration of my faith. (Check!) Three—commit to being a partner

What is the condition of the heart that divides the Body of Christ over the act of a ritual?

by investing in what God is doing through the church. (OK . . . I'm in.)

So I've read through this and am getting ready to sign; and then it starts to gnaw at me. I was baptized as an infant according to my Catholic upbringing. But is that what they mean? Are they talking about a water baptism to include submersion? One that is done as a decision made after the "age of consent"? I've never done that! What do I do? Does that mean I can't be a "partner" in this church? Am I really saved?! Am I going to go to heaven?!! Stand back . . . I'm gonna' pop!!! (Moment to breathe . . .)

After talking with one the elders about not being "baptized"; I was told it was not a disqualifying issue for membership and then it was dropped. BUT NOT FOR ME! I'm not getting off the hook that easily! OH NO! Not letting this go!

So I set out on a search for answers. What does it mean to be "baptized"? Heck, I had even heard someone say that it was Christ's commandment to be baptized. The questions just kept building up and I wanted to know if I needed to be baptized after nearly 25 years of "being saved"! Was I being disobedient to Jesus Christ because I had not been baptized?

When I first started researching to write on this subject; the first direction I started was down the philosophical, theological, biblical . . . seminary, Bible College, "I'm going to set you people straight" approach. (Whew! That was a mouthful.) I researched the Word (Bible-for those of you who are new to the program). I studied from "Systematic Theology" by Wayne Grudem; which is a textbook in many Bible Colleges. I got my hands on "The Documents of Vatican II" which is a comprehensive copy of the 16 Documents of Vatican II (that's for all the Catholic's). I took a thorough approach on solving this dilemma once and for all. After all, this very topic had divided entire religious communities! Denominations have been split and with strict interpretation of each denominations beliefs; how and when you had been baptized could be the difference between Heaven and Hell! . . . WHAT?!

After much research, much study and a whole lot of prayer; I came to a very clear conclusion as to what I feel the Bible has to say about Baptism. And what I have found will certainly anger a lot of people, shock a few, and just plain confuse most; but hear it goes.

I hate to go all WWJD on everybody; but as I looked closer at this subject, the question as well as the answers just kept coming to this: What would Jesus do? This is what I found:

In John chapter 8; a woman who had committed adultery was brought before Jesus and as per the law was to be stoned. Jesus did not question the law, he questioned their hearts. "Let him who is without sin among you be the first to throw a stone at her."

In Matthew chapter 5; Jesus delivered what has become known as the beatitudes which over simply put, is an instruction on the condition of a humble heart.

In Matthew chapter 6; Jesus is instructing his disciples on giving to the poor, praying and fasting. "Beware of practicing your righteousness before other people in order to be seen by them, for then you will have no reward from your Father who is in heaven." Jesus strictly warns against public displays and charges them with the importance of the condition of their heart in their relationship with their Heavenly Father.

In Mark chapter 2 and into chapter 3; the Scribes and the Pharisees are challenging Jesus with the Law regarding; healing outside the law, not honoring the law on fasting, harvesting grain on the Sabbath and healing on the Sabbath. Jesus again did not challenge the law, but he challenged their hearts in their application of the law.

In Matthew chapter 13; again the Scribes and Pharisees are challenging Jesus for his disciples not keeping the "traditions" of the elders. Again, Jesus responds by challenging their hearts and quotes scripture: "This people honors me with their lips, but their heart is far from me; in vain do they worship me, teaching as doctrines the commandments of men."

Jesus goes on to issue the "seven woes" to the Scribes and the Pharisees in Matthew chapter 23 which are all about the condition of the heart and actions verses real relationship with their Heavenly Father.

In Matthew chapter 4, Mark chapter's 1 and 2, Luke chapter 5 and John chapter 1: When Jesus called and invited his disciples there was no ceremonies, no rituals, no requirements; it was simply, "follow me".

I could go on and on giving examples of how Jesus handled different situations as he encountered them, but it ultimately all comes down to the question of rituals versus relationships; the condition of your heart. Now here is where some of you start revving up your engines and your blood begins to boil. "So you're against baptisms then". You'll cross your arms, squint your eyes, set your jaw, look down at me (my favorite part), and quote me "the Great Commission" in Matthew 28:19 where Jesus says; "Go therefore and make disciples of all nations, **baptizing** them in the name of the Father and the Son and the Holy Spirit . . ." Then you tell me it's quoted again in Mark, however not acknowledging that from Mark 16:14 on, is questioned by some Bible scholars as being written by Mark because it is not found in the early manuscripts. You also won't quote or explain Luke's writings in Acts chapter 1 when Jesus told his disciples that; "you heard from me, for John baptized with water, but you will be baptized with the Holy

In proper perspective, baptism is invaluable; out it is a trap!

Spirit not many days from now." You also won't explain to me why there is no recording of Jesus performing any rituals, including a water baptism, anywhere in any scripture or any part of the Bible.

Now, if you think I've gone too far, please stay with me for just a minute. If I have offended you, I sincerely apologize and I beg you to follow me through on this. I want you to understand that I am not against baptisms. I also want you to understand that I believe that being baptized plays a very important role in the maturation of new Christians by making a public declaration of their decision to follow Jesus Christ. I believe that a physical display is invaluable in helping to cement the reality of the spiritual decision that is being made. I also understand that as broken and sinful human beings, we need such rituals to make our decisions real to us and to remind us of the commitment we are making or have made.

However; I just want to make clear as Paul wrote in many of his letters. We are justified by faith, not through an act, behavior or ritual. Just as the act of a baptism, the act of circumcision, or display of spiritual gifts cannot guarantee your salvation. Any more than by not being baptized, circumcised or displaying spiritual gifts can prevent your salvation.

> *The goal of evangelism is a relationship, not a ritual!*

Listen very carefully here. I am not writing this to cause dissention, arguments or controversy. I am not advocating one practice over another or placing one denomination or even one religion over another. I am simply pointing out that your Heavenly Father; our Lord Jesus Christ is simply seeking a relationship with you.

If you are feeling led or an urge to be baptized and in that act it assists you in a better understanding of your relationship with Jesus Christ and furthers your growth. Run, don't walk, to the nearest body of water and be baptized. Submerge yourself into what it is to die with Christ and be raised again as a new creature. Know what it is to be washed clean of all your sins and come out of the water a new son or daughter of our Lord and Heavenly Father, Jesus Christ. In that baptism I urge you to pray for the baptism of the Holy Spirit; pray for all the power, blessings and strength that God has for you in the Holy Spirit. Do it, and do it soon!

But caution to anyone who mandates a ritual. For then we become those same Scribes and Pharisees that knew and practiced the law, but did not understand what it was to have a relationship with their creator, their Lord, their Heavenly Father; Jesus Christ.

May all the blessings and love of our Heavenly Father be with you always. May we walk in love as we all continue in our daily struggle against flesh to grow; not only in our understanding, but in our relationship with the one who sacrificed all; so that the penalty for our sins are paid. It is by His grace and in His name we pray; Amen.

I WAS THINKING . . .

Is my relationship with my Heavenly Father and the faith in that relationship based on a ritual?

Do I look at others and place judgment on them based on their fruit; or whether or not they have performed from a checklist?

What is Jesus Christ calling me to do?

Is my faith founded and based on a ritual or a relationship?

WHAT IS FASTING

I find it very ironic; just a few moments ago, while I was taking a break from researching to write this, I was chuckling to myself as I was eating cake and ice cream that was left over from my wife's birthday. Cake and ice cream while I write about fasting; keep that in mind about my own shortcomings as we continue forward. Know that I am not perfect and know also that my writing has done more for me and my search for greater understanding and greater relationship with my Heavenly Father than it will probably do for you! But I go on.

So let's begin by defining what fasting was in biblical times; that is, let's put them into the context in which they were written. First of all, I must say that I could not find anything written in the Bible that specifically defines what fasting is; nor could I find any specific verses outlining how fasting was to be performed. So I will give you the references that I have found outlining how it was used then. I'm sure there are some great biblical scholars who will undoubtedly refute some of the details of what I have to say; and to them I say I welcome your knowledge, your insight and your wisdom. Write a book.

Why there was fasting?

In biblical times, that is to say the times of the writings of the Old Testament, leading up to and through the writings of the New Testament, fasting was used for several reasons. For instance, fasting was used as a social custom as a standard part of mourning the death of a loved one. Depriving yourself of food was a way of showing your grief and sense of loss. When the Philistines defeated the army of Saul on Mt. Gilboa; Saul's family had all fallen and he took his own life. All the bodies were collected, "And they buried their bones under the oak in Jabesh and fasted for seven days." (1 Chronicles 10:12)

Fasting was used as a way of offering confession and supplication. Samuel called all of Israel to repent for their idolatry and; "So they gathered at Mizpah and drew water and poured it out before the LORD and fasted on that day and said there, 'We have sinned against the Lord.'" (1 Samuel 7:6) This passage also alludes to the pouring out of water being in addition to fasting food, water being the additional sacrifice. In the 9th chapter of Nehemiah vs. 1-5; Israel spent the day fasting, confessing, worshiping, praying and reading from the "Book of the Law of the Lord".

Fasting was used as a way to offer up humility, prayer or emphasize the need for intervention. In 2 Samuel 12:16, David fasted in hopes of saving his son from death. In Ezra 8:21-23, Ezra declared a fast, "that we might humble ourselves before our God, to seek from him a safe journey . . ." on their way back to Jerusalem. In Ezra chapter 9, she fasted and prayed for guidance in dealing with interracial marriages. Nehemiah 1:4 was a prayer for the distress and destruction that was going on in Jerusalem. Esther chapter 4 describes fasting and prayer for protection from Haman in Persia who vowed to kill all the Jews.

How did they fast?

"Now on the twenty-fourth day of this month the people of Israel were assembled with fasting and in sackcloth, and with earth on their heads. And the Israelites separated themselves from all foreigners and stood and confessed their sins and the iniquities of their fathers. And they stood up in their place and read from the Book of the Law of the Lord, their God for a quarter of the day; for another quarter of it they made confession and worshiped the Lord their God . . ." (Nehemiah 9:1-3). King Darius, when faced with knowing he would have to cast Daniel into the lion's den; "Then the king went to his palace and spent the night fasting; no diversions were brought to him, and sleep fled from him." (Daniel 6:18) Daniel prayed for his people, "Then I turned my face to the Lord God, seeking him by prayer and pleas for mercy with fasting and sackcloth and ashes. I prayed to the Lord my God and made confession . . ." (Daniel 9:3-4)

Fasting was a way to show mourning, reverence and humility or repentance. Also, fasting was used to seek Gods help, guidance, or forgiveness. Fasting was performed by abstaining from food for a single meal or up to several days. Typical ritual fasting was done for 1 day at a time on pre-designated days. Refraining from water would be an added deprivation. In most instances of fasting was included wearing of sackcloth which would be comparable to burlap; an attempt to deprive the body of further comfort. The covering the head with dirt or ash also contributed to decreased comfort. This all was to show an act of depriving self of comfort in a display of humility before the Lord.

In the New Testament, the 4 Gospels refer to fasting on several occasions. In Matthew the 4th chapter, Jesus fasted for 40 days in the desert. In the book of Acts, at the church at Antioch, it was during fasting and prayer that the Holy Spirit called Barnabas and Saul into service. Acts 14:23, fasting and prayer was conducted over the elders selected for the church.

There are also multiple warnings against fasting improperly. The Bible cautions multiple times about true and false fasting; against fasting for ritual or appearance verses fasting in righteousness: Zachariah 7:1-14, Isaiah 58, Hosea 6:6 and Jesus warns us in Matthew 6:16-18.

Fasting is not mentioned much in any of the letters of the New Testament; however, there are many references to self-discipline and self-control. Galatians 5:23 mentions self-control as one of the fruits of the Spirit. In 1st Timothy 3:2, Paul lists self-control as a quality of overseers. In 2 Timothy 1:7 Paul writes, "God gave us a spirit not of fear but of power and love and self-control." In 2 Timothy 3, Paul lists lack of self-control as one of the signs of Godlessness in the last days. In Titus, self-control is listed multiple times in the 1st and second chapter as positive qualities.

I hope that I haven't muddied the waters with attempting to give a little history of where and how fasting was used in the Bible. The real question is, do we fast today and how do we go about doing it.

Fasting in today's world.

It is mentioned throughout the Bible of our struggle between our spirit and our flesh; our spirit that desires the things of heaven, of service, of eternity and of GOD; and our flesh that desires things of this earth, selfish, self-serving and sinful. In Romans chapter 8 and Galatians chapter 5; Paul clearly outlines the differences in the results of either focusing our attention on our spirit or on our flesh. So how does that apply to fasting today.

When I pray and study about fasting, this is what the spirit says to me. Fasting has 2 necessary and equal elements. (1) The physical: depriving the body of a desire; and (2) the spiritual: spending that time in prayer. Let me explain:

The Physical—Denying the flesh:

The first element of fasting is about self-discipline and self-control. It is us taking control of our will and telling our flesh NO! In a world today where addiction, laziness, self-service, fast service, obesity, health problems and so on; we have become a people lacking in self-control (myself included). "I want it my way and I want it now!" I suggest that any restriction we put on ourselves for any length of time is a needed exercise in self-control. Limiting any self-gratification is always a good exercise, but if you are looking for real spiritual breakthrough, I recommend a total restriction from the world. That is to say **no** food, **no** comforts, **no** electronics and **no** distractions; shut it all down! Start with just a few hours and 1 meal, build up to and shoot for 24 hrs. (If you have health problems, please take that into consideration.)

Humble yourself before the Lord, deprive yourself before the Lord. The point is to take your focus off things of this world, to take your focus off your physical needs, wants and desires.

The Spiritual—prayer:

During your time of fasting, it is most important to spend that time in prayer. If you're not sure how to pray, use the example Jesus gave us in Matthew 6. Acknowledge God for who He is, give Him praise and worship, ask for forgiveness for the things that you have done, let him know your needs and ask Him for His help, and thank Him for all that He has done for you. In your time of fasting, spend time in His Word. Read the Bible for crying out loud! It is the Living Word of God and the Spirit will speak to you through it! If you're still uncertain about prayer, for the love of peanut butter and jelly . . . just talk to Him. Your Heavenly Father just wants to hear from you!

These are the 2 elements necessary for a fast. Separately; they are good for you and will give you positive direction for your life. Exercise them together and I promise you a real spiritual awakening.

How long should you fast?
Fasting is exercised in many ways today. Around the time of Lent, people will fast by giving up a small portion of their fleshly desires for that season; generally 40 days. I guess just let me be succinct; If you have identified (or the spirit has brought to your attention) an area of your life you need to get under control; STOP IT. Declaring you're going to stop deserts for a week and then return to the same habit is hardly a productive exercise. If the spirit lays it on your heart to stop something you're doing; STOP IT! The common response I hear is "I can't". Listen; I love you, your Father in Heaven loves you; but you can stop, you just don't want to. (OUCH . . . that was personal!)

Go to your Father in prayer, spend some time fasting, be willing to listen to and follow what the Spirit has to say to you. You will find that you are capable of so much more than you have or will ever realize.

Jesus looked at them and said, "With man it is impossible, but not with GOD. For all things are possible with GOD." (Mark 10:27)

For those who have never spent time in fasting and prayer, they will tell you that it is not a necessary part of your spiritual walk. For those who have, they will tell you that they wouldn't be where they are without it. For me, I will tell you that you can never spend too much time with your Father; and sometimes it is necessary to shut off the world, shut off your flesh, and just spend a little time with Him.

Remember, you rule your flesh; your thoughts, your wants and your desires, they do not rule you! Take time to tell yourself no and your Heavenly Father WILL honor that! May God the Father and creator of all . . . bless your time of fasting, your heart of worship and your sacrifices of self.

Your Father is calling!

I WAS THINKING . . .

When I spend time in prayer, am I reciting words or engaged in communication; engaged in a relationship?

Am I willing to sacrifice a little of myself and a little of my time after all that Jesus Christ sacrificed for me?

Am I disappointed in a relationship that I have not invested in? (That one hit's a little close to the vest!)

QUESTIONS OF PURGATORY

Well, I have found it to be difficult that when you spend any length of time discussing religion or theology, the subject of purgatory will also eventually come up. Being the opinionated man than I am, and to those that know me, I always have something to say (about everything); I feel obligated to attempt to give an answer to this question as well.

I was raised Catholic and even spent a summer at a Seminary School as I searched out the possibility of becoming a Catholic Priest. So to just give you an understanding of my upbringing and foundation; I was brought up in the Catholic faith and did complete all my sacraments. My full Catholic name is Michael Joseph Paul; talk about having names to live up to!

So anyway; the Catholic Church strongly believes in the concept of purgatory. There are several versus and references used to support this ideology. One is in the second book of Maccabees. (Before I go on, I must clarify that Christians outside the Catholic Church consider the book of Maccabees to be part of the Apocrypha, which is considered to be useful Hebrew text but not part of the accepted canonized texts of the Bible; however the books of Maccabees is included in the texts canonized by the Catholic Church.) In the 12th chapter of 2 Maccabees, Judas Maccabees had just led his army in victory against an opposing army led by Gorgias, governor of Idumea. After honoring the Sabbath, Judas went to collect and bury the dead per their custom. Upon recovering the dead he found each of them to be wearing an amulet sacred to a false idol Jamnia which was forbidden under Jewish law. They determined that because of their sin, that is why they had been slain during the battle. Judas then "took up a collection among all his soldiers, amounting to two thousand silver drachmas, which he sent to Jerusalem to provide for an expiatory sacrifice." (2 Maccabees 12:43) "Thus he made atonement for the dead that they might be freed from this sin." (2 Maccabees 12:46) This reference is made to point to the possibility of a place between heaven and hell where sins could be atoned.

Ludwig Ott (Fundamentals of Catholic Dogma) writes that purgatory is the place where the souls of believers go to be further purified from sin until they are ready to be admitted into heaven.

Scripture used is in Revelations 21:27, speaking of heaven; "But nothing unclean will ever enter it, nor anyone who does what is detestable or false, but only those who are written in the Lamb's book of life." This passage is used to state that we are born of sin, live in a world of sin and therefore we are unclean and suggests that we must first be cleansed before we can enter into the Holiness of God's presence, suggesting a need for a place like purgatory.

Other scriptures for your reference are; Mathew 12:31-36, 2 Corinthians 5:10, Revelations 20:12-13, 1 Peter 1:15-17 all point to a day of judgment. These are used to imply that with judgment, there will be a punishment which is used to imply a need for purgatory.

Those who do not believe in purgatory point to some of the following scriptures: Paul writes in the 2 Corinthians 5:1-10 referring to our Heavenly dwelling; "we would rather be away from the body and at home with the lord." (2Cor 5:8) Paul writes to the church at Philippi (Philippians 1:18-30) while he was in prison. He was torn in his desire to serve in this life and his desire to be with Jesus in heaven. My favorite is in Luke 23:42; Jesus is hanging on the cross between two thieves, only one of which who recognized him as the Son of God. He simply asked Jesus to remember him and Jesus replied, "Truly I say to you, ***today*** you will be with me in paradise." "For God so loved the world, that he gave his only Son, that whoever believed in him should not perish but have eternal life." (John 3:16)

My parents are Catholic and I have close relationships with a lot of people who believe whole heartedly in the idea of purgatory. Some have even adapted to believe that purgatory does exist but it happens in an instance at the moment of death as we enter into the presence of God.

This is what I believe; God is a just God, and where there is justice, there is choice and consequence. I believe there will be a day of judgment and we will stand accountable for every act, every thought and every word. I also believe in Jesus Christ. I believe he was sent by my Father to bear the punishment for my sins and in Him I have been made righteous. I am not righteous nor am I free or clean of sin. But in Jesus Christ, I have been cleansed and made worthy to enter into the kingdom and the presence of my Father. "For as by the one man's disobedience (Adam) the many were made sinners, so by the one man's obedience (Jesus) the many will be made righteous." (Romans 5:19)

I would further add that almost all Christians believe in some form of cleansing, passage or purgatory on our way to heaven. I will also add that in God, there is no concept of time. Who is to say how "long" this transformation process is between our time here on earth and what waits for us in Heaven?

In finishing, this is what I want you to take away from this. I am not here to praise or condemn one opinion or the other. Maybe I have given you some references to further your own research. If anyone that would tell you of your own salvation based on your belief on this subject should further search their own heart. If this subject is stumbling block for you; earnestly pray, prayerfully read, and ask the Holy Spirit to grant you discernment and peace. As our search is not for wisdom and answers; our ultimate goal is to seek a better understanding and a closer relationship with our Father.

May the Grace and Peace beyond understanding be with you as you further pursue a better understanding of God's plan for you in this life and may all of God's blessing be with us as we seek and desire a greater relationship with HIM!

I WAS THINKING . . .

Does resolving this issue in my own mind and heart bring me to a closer relationship with my Heavenly Father, or is it a distraction?

When I discuss theology with those that have differing opinions, am I more concerned about furthering my own "rightness" or furthering their relationship?

Am I ready to stand under the judgment of God today or do I need to reflect on my own relationship, my own heart and my own actions? If so, what am I waiting for?

"SPEAKING IN TONGUES"

Well, I certainly don't shy away from the "hot topics", do I? I find myself writing on a topic that is disconcerting, only in the fact that I know that it is a very highly disputed subject. It breaks my heart to know that there are entire denominations that can't get along, based solely on this one topic! But I have felt it necessary to at least address the issue in that it's a subject that will inevitably come up when I'm talking to new or young believers. I hope that this is a good resource for you to search out answers for yourself as you deliberate on the question, or as a resource for you to help others. Either way, I hope that I can give you some clarity or at least "food for thought" on the subject.

I have attempted to keep as much of this a collection of verses from the Bible so as to keep it in perspective of what the Holy Bible says and less of "my opinion". That is the reason for the odd format, so if you can bear with me; let's get started!

GIFTS OF THE HOLY SPIRIT
1 Corinthians 12:4-11 ESV

Now there are varieties of gifts, but the same Spirit; and there are varieties of service, but the same Lord; and there are varieties of activities, but it is the same God who empowers them all in everyone. To each is given the manifestation of the Spirit for the common good. For to one is given through the Spirit the utterance of wisdom, and to another the utterance of knowledge

according to the same Spirit, to another faith by the same Spirit, to another a gifts of healing by the one Spirit, to another the working of miracles, to another prophecy, to another the ability to distinguish between spirits, **to another various kinds of tongues**, to another the interpretation of tongues. **All these are empowered by one and the same Spirit, who apportions to each one individually as he wills.**
1 Corinthians 12:4-6 KJ

Now there are diversities of gifts, but the same Spirit. And there are differences of administrations, but the same Lord. And there are diversities of operations, but it is the same God which worketh all in all.

JOE'S NOTE: There are many gifts of the Holy Spirit and I don't think Paul intended that this be the entire list, but these are the gifts he chooses to list when speaking to the church in Corinth. Paul is simply saying there are many gifts of the Holy Spirit and only by the Spirit are these gifts "empowered" on an individual basis. All are gifts of the Holy Spirit, NOT REQUIREMENTS!

WHAT IS TONGUES
1 Corinthians 14: ESV

For one who speaks in a tongue speaks not to men but to God; for no one understands him, but he **utters mysteries in the Spirit**. For if I pray in a tongue, my spirit prays but my mind is unfruitful.

JOE'S NOTE: Paul makes it clear; speaking in tongues is for the understanding of your spirit and GOD. Not for the understanding of others, NOT EVEN FOR THE UNDERSTANDING OF YOUR OWN MIND.

TONGUES IN PUBLIC OR IN CHURCH
1 Corinthians 14: 6-19 ESV

Now, brothers, if I come to you speaking in tongues, how will I benefit you unless I bring you some revelation or knowledge or prophecy or teaching? If even lifeless instruments, such as the flute or the harp, do not give distinct notes, how will anyone know what is played? And if the bugle gives an indistinct sound, who will get ready for battle? So with yourselves, if with your tongue you utter speech that is not intelligible, how will anyone know what is said? For you will be speaking into the air. There are doubtless many different languages in the world, and none is without meaning, but if I do not know the meaning of the language, I will be a foreigner to the speaker and the speaker a foreigner to me. So with yourselves, since you are eager for manifestations of the Spirit, strive to excel in building up the church.
Therefore, one who speaks in a tongue should pray for the power to interpret. **For if I pray in a tongue, my spirit prays but my mind is unfruitful.** What am I to do? I will pray with my spirit, but I will pray with my mind also; I will sing praise with my spirit, but I will sing with my mind also. Otherwise, if you give thanks with your spirit, how can anyone in the position of an outsider say "Amen" to your thanksgiving when he does not know what you are saying? For you may be giving thanks well enough, but the other person is not being built up. I thank God that I speak in tongues more than all of you. Nevertheless, in church I would rather speak five words with my mind in order to instruct others, than ten thousand words in a tongue.

JOE'S NOTE: The churches purpose is to prophecy; that is to instruct, to teach, to share the Word of God, to educate, to impart spiritual and biblical knowledge. And to prophesy; that is to build up, to lift up, to encourage, and to inspire. Speaking or praying in tongues is for the edification of *your* spirit, not the church body. Paul says clearly that he is thankful to God that he speaks tongues more than all he is addressing, yet he says equally as clear, [for the edification of the church, for the prophecy and prophesy of the church] he would rather speak five words with his mind (with his mouth in an intelligible language) than ten thousand words in a tongue (that no one may understand or be edified by).

GOD IS A GOD OF ORDER
1 Corinthians 14:26-40 ESV

What then, brothers? When you come together, each one has a hymn, a lesson, a revelation, a tongue, or an interpretation. Let all things be done for building up. If any speak in a tongue, let there be only two or at most three, and each in turn, and let someone interpret. But if there is no one to interpret, let each of them keep silent in church and speak to himself and to God. Let two or three prophets speak, and let the others weigh what is said. If a revelation is made to another sitting there, let the first be silent. For you can all prophesy one by one, so that all may learn and all be encouraged, and the spirits of prophets are subject to prophets. For God is not a God of confusion but of peace.

As in all the churches of the saints, the women should keep silent in the churches. For they are not permitted to speak, but should be in submission, as the Law also says. If there is anything they desire to learn, let them ask their husbands at home. For it is shameful for a woman to speak in church.

Or was it from you that the word of God came? Or are you the only ones it has reached? If anyone thinks that he is a prophet, or spiritual, he should acknowledge that the things I am writing to you are a command of the Lord. If anyone does not recognize this, he is not recognized. So, my brothers, earnestly desire to prophesy, and do not forbid speaking in tongues. But all things should be done decently and in order.

CAN TONGUES BE INTERPRETTED
JOE'S NOTE: Yes, Paul speaks directly to that in his letter to the church in Corinth. But he clearly defines this ability as a separate gift that should be prayed for and sought after. But again, remember that not all the church body will possess all gifts so that no one should speak out loud in tongues with the assumption that there is someone present who can interpret.

COMMON MISCONCEPTION
The gift of tongues was first introduced with the imparting or gift of the Holy Spirit.
Acts 2:1-4 ESV

When the day of Pentecost arrived, they were all together in one place. And suddenly there came from heaven a sound like a mighty rushing wind, and it filled the entire house where they were sitting. And divided tongues as of fire appeared to them and rested on each one of them. And they were all filled with the Holy Spirit and began to speak in other tongues as the Spirit gave them utterance.

JOE'S NOTE: It was this point when all the apostles were gathered and the Holy Spirit came upon them, blessed them with, and imparted upon them supernatural (1. Not of natural world; relating to or attributed to phenomena that cannot be explained by natural laws. 2. Relating to deity {Encarta Dictionary}) gifts of the Holy Spirit (discussed in 1 Corinthians 12) and from here they set out imparting supernatural wisdom, knowledge, faith, healing, working of miracles, prophecy, etc . . . The gift of tongues was just one of the supernatural abilities granted to the apostles by the Holy Spirit.

Now enter the confusion: paragraph 2 of Acts chapter 2.
Acts 2:5-13 *ESV*

Now there were dwelling in Jerusalem Jews, devout men from every nation under heaven. And at this sound the multitude came together, and they were bewildered, because each one was hearing them speak in his own language. And they were amazed and astonished, saying, "Are not all these who are speaking Galileans? And how is it that we hear, each of us in his own native language? Parthians and Medes and Elamites and residents of Mesopotamia, Judea and Cappadocia, Pontus and Asia, Phrygia and Pamphylia, Egypt and the parts of Libya belonging to Cyrene, and visitors from Rome, both Jews and proselytes, Cretans and Arabians—we hear them telling in our own tongues the mighty works of God." And all were amazed and perplexed, saying to one another, "What does this mean?" But others mocking said, "They are filled with new wine."

JOE'S NOTE: First I ask you to try to take a moment to put yourself in that place and in that time; observing as an outsider, a non-Christian, and witnessing what was going on with the Holy Spirit through the disciples. What a total sense of bewilderment, amazement, confusion and WOW!

Understand there were a lot of miracles occurring at this time, but we are just going to talk about tongues. Paul say's in 1 Corinthians that he who speaks in tongues, speaks in his spirit to GOD and not to man, that only his spirit and GOD understand. This would explain why some there in Jerusalem thought the disciples were "filled with wine" due to the strange utterances. But there were also many visitors from other countries who were not Christians or even Jews, who heard the disciples preaching "in his own language", "the mighty works of God". The disciples were preaching, and all present "hear them telling in our own tongues (language)". This is yet another miracle. Were the disciple's speaking in tongues and the Holy Spirit imparted to all present the gift to interpret their tongues, or were the disciples preaching in their own language and the Holy Spirit interceded to allow all to understand? I don't know and you know, those present at the time probably didn't know the answer to that either. **Who are we to speak on the power of the Holy Spirit?**

DIVISION

For more than two thousand years, there has been controversy over the gifts of the Holy Spirit and speaking more directly to the gift of speaking in tongues. Paul had to address it when writing to the Church at Corinth due to mishandling of the gift, and churches have been divided on this issue to this day. There are two camps of people within the Christian community; one who think that the gift of tongues was for the Apostles, to be used by them as a sign of the presence of the Holy Spirit as they spread the Gospel of Jesus Christ, and that the gift of tongues died with the Apostles. The other side believes that the gift exists to this day. The argument is further confused on how you wish to interpret the following scripture: 1 Corinthians 13:8; "As for prophecies, they will pass away; as for tongues, they will cease; as for knowledge, it will pass away". But I will put this passage into context shortly.

JOE'S PARABLE

I came from a small town of Lima, Ohio. One of the things that everyone from Lima will brag about is a local restaurant called Kewpee's, and I am telling you that it is the best hamburger you will ever eat. When I was in the military and stationed in Texas for schooling, I ran across someone that was not from Lima, but had been to Lima and we immediately began talking about the Kewpee burger. We tried to tell those around us how good this burger was and they either chose to accept that it was the best hamburger ever, or they didn't. When it comes down to it, the Kewpee burger cannot be explained, it has to be experienced. The Holy Spirit and the gift of tongues is the same. I can try to describe it and you can choose to accept it or reject it. But in the end, it cannot be explained, it has to be experienced.

SO WHAT DO WE DO?

JUDGEMENT

I wrote in an earlier thought, we are called to love. We are not to judge. If you believe in tongues, and others don't; love and do not judge. If you don't believe in tongues and others do; love and do not judge. We should all give praise and be blessed for the individual gifts and talents that we have been granted by God and the Holy Spirit. We should give equal praise for the blessings, gifts and talents that God and the Holy Spirit have given to others. For as we have been granted our gifts so that we may serve and others may be blessed, so much more others have been given gifts so that we may be blessed.

HOW TO MOVE FORWARD-PERSUE LOVE
1 Corinthians 13 ESV

If I speak in the tongues of men and of angels, but have not love, I am a noisy gong or a clanging cymbal. And if I have prophetic powers, and understand all mysteries and all knowledge, and if I have all faith, so as to remove mountains, but have not love, I am nothing. If I give away all I have, and if I deliver up my body to be burned, but have not love, I gain nothing.

Love is patient and kind; love does not envy or boast; it is not arrogant or rude. It does not insist on its own way; it is not irritable or resentful; it does not rejoice at wrongdoing, but rejoices with the truth. Love bears all things, believes all things, hopes all things, endures all things.

Love never ends. As for prophecies, they will pass away; as for tongues, they will cease; as for knowledge, it will pass away. For we know in part and we prophesy in part, but when the perfect (Jesus) comes, the partial will pass away. When I was a child, I spoke like a child, I thought like a child, I reasoned like a child. When I became a man, I gave up childish ways. For now we see in a mirror dimly, but then face to face. Now I know in part; then I shall know fully, even as I have been fully known. So now faith, hope, and love **abide** *(to dwell, to live or reside in a place-Encarta Dictionary)*, these three; but the greatest of these is love.

DESIRING SPIRITUAL GIFTS

Paul encourages us in 1 Corinthians 14:1—Pursue love, and earnestly desire the spiritual gifts, especially that you may prophesy [build up, lift up, encourage, inspire].

If you desire any gift, or all of the gifts of the Holy Spirit, I encourage you to earnestly pursue and pray in faith. But to pray in faith is to believe. If you do not believe in a spiritual gift, the Holy Spirit cannot grant you a gift in which you do not truly believe.

I pray that you continually seek a deeper relationship and a deeper understanding of your Heavenly Father. Always pursue wisdom only under the guides of pursuing a greater intimacy with your creator. Seek understanding only while joined always with the search for truth. Desire to show love when confronted with those that may disagree. And let the Holy Spirit always be your guide.

I WAS THINKING . . .

Does God have something waiting for me that I cannot receive simply because I refuse to believe?

In my own search, am I more concerned about the truth or about being right?

Can I stand firm in my belief while still demonstrating the love of Christ; in other words, can I disagree without being disagreeable?

Am I about issues, or about relationships?

TODAYS SERMON

I used this particular title as I reflect on where I am today and where I have come from. What I am referring to, is spending time in awe and joy over where God has brought me in my spiritual growth and maturity. I am dumfounded and even embarrassed at the philosophies and theologies that I have clung to in the past and what I have come to understand as truth today. I am just enamored at the evolution of my understanding and the growth in my intimacy with my Heavenly Father. I call this "Today's Sermon" because that is where God has my heart today as I anxiously await where he will have me tomorrow.

I was part of a conversation among good, honest, solid Christian men. As in any time where earnest believers are gathered together and sharing on their faith, discussing Jesus Christ, (always AWSOME) and attempting to sort through the struggles of everyday life in Christ; the conversation that day hit on the topic of what should be preached from the pulpit related to specific subjects. Now I am not going to bring up the specifics of that discussion. I will however note that these conversations are always born out of one of the hot topics of the day, usually social topics in nature.

That conversation sent my mind into overdrive. My mind couldn't stop toiling over the "sermon" that I would like to hear on Sunday morning. I know that this is quit self-serving; but after all, this *is* my book. So anyway, my ideal Sunday morning sermon would go a little something like this:

There is a great and powerful creator; one that existed before time, one that existed before and created space itself. Nothing existed before it was created by God. There was nothing that existed before Him, and there will be nothing that lasts beyond Him. God has created all! In the vastness of the universe and all that exists, God took the time to create a one-time only, one of a kind, unique being . . . you. God took the time to create you out of a most profound act of love. Out of that profound act of a magnificent creation, all he asks of you is a relationship. He wants to know you; He wants you to know Him.

God so wants to get to know you and is offering Himself to you to the extent that he wants to spend an eternity with you. Not a lifetime, but an eternity. Here is the catch; His love is so great that He will not force this relationship on you. Though it is in His power to create all, in any way that He wants, in his infinite love God has granted you free will. God has given you a choice. You don't **have** to do anything.

Now understand that God is a perfect God and a God of perfect order. Everything has been designed perfectly. Everything has been designed so perfectly and yet so complex that science has been defining and calculating and categorizing everything around us for centuries. In this perfect design, there are laws. Laws of nature, laws of science, laws of motion and so on. Newton, Einstein, Galileo, Copernicus all wrestled with the perfect order and design of creation.

There is one law that we all operate under and we all have an understanding of, but for the life of me, I couldn't find it mentioned as a specific law anywhere! What I am speaking of is the law of relationships. There are rules, or laws if you will, that govern how we act in relationship to one another. Rules that if adhered to draw us into closer relationship, and rules that if violated drive us apart. Examples: If you get married and continue to date around, you will not stay married very long. If you have a girlfriend and you kiss another girl, no more girlfriend. If you physically or emotionally abuse someone you are in relationship with, you destroy the relationship.

Now there are thousands of books written on relationships, marriage, parenting and the like. Everyone and his brother have an opinion on how to improve on all the various relationships we find ourselves in life. But what they all agree on is there are laws.

Now with all laws and rules come consequences. If you violate the rules . . . there are consequences. Once again, obeying the laws of relationship draw you closer; violating the laws of relationship drive you apart. To some this may be oversimplified, but I believe it really is this simple. This is where things begin to get a little scary. These laws of relationship apply to God as well. (I will allow a minute for all the air to return into the room after the gasps.)

Here's the deal, God created us to have free will. In that free will He understands that allows us choice and inevitably when given choices, bad decisions will be made—sin. Sin, I am going to simply define for you as any decision that violates the law of relationship between you and God. Now God being of perfect order understands that we will, by design, violate those laws of relationship and we will sin. Now in understanding that choice does not exist without consequences (again another pause to allow that to sink in, you may need to read that again . . . take your time), God has already paid the consequences of your violations through the sacrifice of His son Jesus Christ.

Recap: Laws of relationship; you are either moving towards a greater relationship or moving towards separation. Laws of choice and consequence; every choice gives you a positive or negative consequence. There is one last law I want to discuss and that is the law of what the Bible refers to as your fruit. To make it very simple; your actions reflect your heart. Saying you are in a relationship while violating all the laws of relationship means . . . you are NOT in relationship.

I started out searching for which bible verses I would use in this. I very quickly realized from the Genesis to Revelations, that the entire Bible is about the joys and the consequences of either being in or out of relationship with our Creator, our God, our Heavenly Father.

The message of *this* sermon is this: If you are violating Gods laws and/or Gods commandments, you are violating the laws of the relationship. If you are living in relationship with your Heavenly Father, it will change you and you will desire to be in greater relationship, which means submission to relationship in Him; submission to His authority, His rule, His laws.

Jesus Christ came to pay the price, to pay the consequences of our sins, our decisions that violated our relationship with God. He did not come so that we could dance on His grave and then pull out our "get out of jail free card". To know Jesus Christ, to know your Heavenly Father is to live in relationship. One prayer, one statement, one act of a ritual is not going to get it done.

Your salvation is freely given by the grace of God; not by your works (or your actions), but by faith that is solidified in your relationship. My warning today is this: If you consider yourself a Christian and you are living your life in violation of the laws of relationship with your Heavenly Father; your day of judgment is going to be a very bad day. (Matthew 7:21-23)

Pray with me; Heavenly Father, I know that I have sinned against you and I have violated your laws, your commandments and your will for my life. Father, I know that my heart is weak and I pray for your Holy Spirit to fill me, to guide me, to strengthen me and to teach me as I commit to live every day of my life in greater relationship with you. Amen.

I WAS THINKING . . .

Am I in a ritual or a relationship?

Do I claim to have a relationship with Jesus Christ while my actions clearly violate the laws of that relationship?

Do I claim to love my Heavenly Father while my "fruit", my actions demonstrate contempt?

Is my day of judgment going to be a bad day, or can I faithfully and confidently look forward to a day of glory?

ARMOR
OF
GOD
THOUGHTS

ARMOR OF GOD

You know, my favorite passage of the bible is in Ephesians when Paul talks about the Armor of God. This is a passage that just resonates through me. The use of armor just conjures up in my mind a variety of pictures, scenes and images that span several hundred years of human history.

I have served in the United States Marine Corps, I have served in law enforcement, and I have spent years studying martial arts and have obtained a black belt. So the concept of battle and combat is something I can really relate to.

When you talk about armor, maybe you immediately begin to get images of battle. Not only preparing offensively, but defensively. At least I start to get all kinds of pictures in my head, but they all are related to wars, to battles, to combat and fighting. I think that Paul chose this analogy, not by chance, but very deliberately for he knows that as Christians, we are in a state of constant battle, constant warfare; a never ending fight.

Paul even says in Ephesians 6:12; "For we do not wrestle against flesh and blood, but against the rulers, against the authorities, against the cosmic powers over this present darkness, against the spiritual forces of evil" (*ESV*). Paul is describing for us a battle, a spiritual battle. He then gives us the clues, the hint, the plan on how to be victorious in this battle. He instructs us to; "take unto you the whole armor of God" Ephesians 6:13 (*KJ*). This is when my mind starts to really take off!

The first image that comes to mind, when I hear armor, is that of the Middle Ages Knight. Sitting on a horse, covered in a polished full suit of armor. Head to toe, no skin exposed. What a site! Now understand that to the knight of the Middle Ages, his armor was probably his single most expensive asset. For most, it was probably more expensive than his home. This was it; this is what he invested everything he had into. It was what kept him alive. Being the most expensive thing that he owned, he made sure to take care of it. Also in the consideration of its care, again, it is what protected him; it is again, what kept him alive! If the knight was fortunate enough and wealthy enough to have a couple of servants, he may have 2 or three servants or "squires" whose full time job was the care of his armor.

Now really stop for a minute and gather the whole essence of this in your mind. A knight's only way to make money was to fight wars or battles, sometimes for his king, sometimes just as a knight for hire. But his entire income, his livelihood was dependent on him fighting and surviving combat, surviving battles. His armor was everything to him. Without his armor intact, he would be vulnerable to injury or death. If his armor was not functioning properly and allowing him to move, he could not effectively move to defend attacks or move well enough to attack successfully. A knight made sure his armor was taken care of; he made sure it fit and he made sure it functioned flawlessly. As part of a knights armor was his shield and weapons. Again, these were the things that provided him a way to make a living, but most important to keep him alive! There were no cracks, crevices or dents in the shield. No holes or even weak spots that could leave him vulnerable. His weapons were also well maintained, no rust, always sharpened to a razor fine precision. Failure of a weapon in combat would leave him with the ability to only defend yourself or run . . . .

can't see much running in a suit of armor, would be funny to watch though!

The next image that jumps into my head is that of the Japanese Samurai. Talk about an intimidating suit of armor. To the Japanese, the Samurai was the most feared of all warriors of the time. The word Samurai who's root word means "those who serve in close attendance to nobility". In China and Japan, the Samurai was closely associated with the mid to upper echelons of the warrior class. The fancy full suits of armor would only be worn by the most elite and highest ranking. The suits would sometimes take a lifetime of additions and decorating. The suits were meant primarily for protection, but were also colorful, large, flashy and with masks all made to make the wearer appear more intimidating. These suits were also cherished by the owner and some believed that the suits had a spirit all its own. Some would be handed down from generation to generation. No greater honor than to dawn the suit of an ancestor.

The warrior of Paul's time was no different. Everything that the Roman Legionnaire would have would be for maximum protection, maximum mobility, and maximum effectiveness. The armor and the weapons chosen and cared for could mean the difference between victory and defeat, between life and death. So when he uses the metaphor of putting on the Armor of God, it is not a passive euphemism, it is an accurate depiction of how we need to prepare for our spiritual combat, spiritual battles, for our spiritual survival; maximum protections, maximum survivability, maximum effectiveness against the enemy.

There is no doubt that to any warrior, it is vital to their survival that their armor is maintained. How much time, effort and care do you put into your armor?!

BELT OF TRUTH

So let's talk about our armor!

When we are confronted with the spiritual enemies, Paul calls us to stand firm. We should stand firm knowing that we have put on our spiritual armor having first "fastened on the belt of truth". The King James says; "having your loins girt about with truth". To me that implies protecting what is most easily vulnerable to injury . . . the TRUTH! Know what is true, do not allow yourselves to be deceived with lies, distractions and falsehoods.

"Lead me in your truth and teach me, for you are the God of my salvation" (Psalms 25:5).

"Teach me your way, oh LORD, that I may walk in your truth" (Psalm 86:11).

"Whoever speaks the truth gives honest evidence, but a false witness utters deceit" (proverbs 12:17).

"I did not speak in secret, in a land of darkness . . . . I the LORD speak the truth; I declare what is right" (Isaiah 45:19).

"And the word became flesh and dwelt among us, and we have seen his glory, glory as of the only Son from the Father, full of grace and truth" (John 1:14).

"So Jesus said to the Jews who believed in him, "If you abide in my word, you are truly my disciples, and you will know the truth, and the truth will set you free." (John 8:31-32).

"When the spirit of truth comes, he will guide you into all the truth, for he will not speak on his own authority, but whatever he hears he will speak, and he will declare to you the things that are to come" (John 16:13).

Jesus prayed for us to his father, "Sanctify them in truth; your word is truth. As you sent me into the world, so I have sent them into the world. And for their sake I consecrate myself, that they also may be sanctified in the truth." (John 17:17-19).

So in preparing for battle, start by tightening down your belt, cinch it tight and know that it is firm, know the Word, know what is true.

BREASTPLATE OF RIGHTEOUSNESS

Paul then tells us to "put on the breastplate of righteousness". I believe that it is important to know and be righteous; I found 565 references in the bible to being righteous! Someone thinks being righteous is important!

"Blessed is the man who walks not in the counsel of the wicked, nor stands in the way of sinners, nor sits in the seat of scoffers; but his delight is in the law of the Lord, and on his law he meditates day and night." (Psalms 1:1-2)

"The Lord judges people; judge me oh Lord, according to my righteousness, and according to the integrity that is in me" (Psalms 7:8).

"I will praise you with an upright heart, when I learn your righteous rules" (Psalms 119:7)

"Whoever pursues righteousness and kindness will find life, righteousness and honor" (Proverbs 21:21).

"He who walks righteously and speaks uprightly, who despises the gain of oppressions, who shakes his hands, lest they hold a bribe, who stops his ears from hearing of bloodshed, and shuts his eyes from looking on evil" (Isaiah 33:15).

"If a man is righteous and does what is just and right-if he does not eat upon the mountains or lift up his eyes to the idols of the house of Israel, does not defile his neighbor's wife or approach a woman in her time of menstrual impurity, does not oppress anyone, but restores to the debtor his pledge, commits no robbery, gives his bread to the hungry and covers the naked with a garment, does not lend at interest or take any profit, withholds his hand from injustice, executes true justice between man and man, walks in my statutes, and keeps my rules by acting faithfully-he is righteous, he shall surely live, declares the Lord God." (Ezekiel 18:5-9)

"Seek the LORD, all you humble of the land, who do his just commands; seek righteousness; seek humility; perhaps you may be hidden on the day of the anger of the Lord" (Zephaniah 2:3)

"And they were both righteous before God, walking blamelessly in all the commandments and statutes of the Lord" (Luke 1:6).

"If the end brings me out all right, what is said against me won't amount to anything. If the end brings me out wrong, then ten angels swearing I was right would make no difference".—Abraham Lincoln

Being righteous; the bible goes on and on about righteousness. Paul spends a good part of the beginning of his letter to the Romans talking about righteousness. In my study of Romans, I surmised that Paul was basically saying be right with God. Through the sin of Adam, we have all lost our righteousness with God, and only through the death and resurrection of Jesus Christ, we have all been made righteous again. God does not expect perfection, adversely he expects us to sin. He knows the sinful nature we are born in to. To be righteous is to be right with God. If you make a mistake, atone for it. If you sin against a brother, make it right. If you sin against God, seek forgiveness and seek penance, not as in 3 "Hail Mary's" and 2 "Our Fathers" type penance, but seek to correct the behavior and take steps to prevent the behavior from re-occurring. If you have done, or do something that is not "right", acknowledge it, correct it, and take steps to prevent it. Sometimes the only preventative step you can take is to give it to God and ask for help. But take action!

I may have appeared to be rambling on the subject of righteousness, but in Paul's illustration, it is our breastplate, as in our armor, it is what protects our chest, our vital organs, our heart, our lungs, liver, spleen . . . . VITAL ORGANS! Know that only through Jesus Christ have we been made right again and it is only through God the father, his Son Jesus Christ AND the Holy Spirit can we maintain our righteousness. Paul is saying that it is vital to our survival to be vigilant at making sure that our breastplate of righteousness is strong, free of tears of blemishes and well maintained so that we can be protected from those that oppose us!

Being righteous is not our ticket to salvation, for our salvation is granted and guaranteed through the sacrifice of God our Father, through his son Jesus the Christ, dependent only on our acceptance. However, to walk in unrighteousness, that is to walk in a way that we *know* to be not right with God, is to walk outside of his law. So you ask; "but if my salvation is guaranteed, why do I need to worry about righteousness"! GLAD YOU ASKED!

Why do your parents make rules for you growing up? Why do you make rules for your own children? Are you just trying to make things as difficult as you can for them? Are you just trying to protect them and keep them as safe as possible? Rules; don't run with scissors, stay out of that cabinet, don't go to bad places, those friends are no good for you, be in by curfew, etc.—all in an effort to protect your children. So how much more would the perfect Father, your Father in Heaven want to protect you? How many times have you been in your Bible and started acting like a rebellious teenager as you read things that have convicted you on how you live!? The Bible is the living Word of God, the voice of your Father, the voice of your parent telling you, warning you, guiding you, and protecting you. (See where I'm going with this yet?) When you attempt to be right with God, to live in righteousness, you choose to live within the guidelines that he has laid out to protect you from the enemy (Satan). When you choose to live in an unrighteous way, you choose to violate the rules or the Law that has been handed down by God to guide you and to protect you. You open yourself up to attack, to hurt, to injury, to pain; in addition to offending your creator, your Father.

Example: Don't drink and drive. You choose to ignore the rule; you get in an accident. You or someone else gets injured or maybe killed. Could you get in an accident and be injured without drinking and driving? Could you drink and drive and not get injured? Sure, but by breaking the rule that is put in place for your protection, your risk for injury compound significantly. There is no difference in the application of righteous living as laid down by the Word of God in the Bible.

If I have not been clear enough for you, let me make it simpler. The law of Choices and Consequences! Choose right living, choose righteousness and have righteous rewards. Choose to violate the Law, choose unrighteousness and the consequences are yours and yours alone. Blame God all you want to, but the choice was yours!

Breastplate of Righteousness; for behind it we find protection!

FEET SHOD WITH THE PREPARATION OF THE GOSPEL OF PEACE

Having "your feet shod with the preparation of the gospel of peace" is how Paul tells us we should walk.

"Noah was a righteous man, blameless in his generation. Noah walked with God. (Genesis 6:9)

"You should follow my rules and keep my statutes and walk in them. I am the Lord your God." (Leviticus 18:4)

Think of it again as a journey. How far can you walk barefoot? How far can you walk when you have the appropriate shoes? Would you hike 10 miles in heels? Would you run a marathon in flip-flops? So we should be protecting our feet appropriately for the task at hand so that your journey can not only be made, but successfully completed. A journey completed with the least amount of pain, suffering and no more "blisters" than are necessary. Walking in sin, trouble, despair, hurt, anger, bitterness, deceit only causes us to stumble, stub our toes, cut our feet and hinder our journey. So walk not only in the Gospel, the Good News of Jesus Christ, but in our preparation, our knowledge, or faith in the Gospel, so that our journey can be great and long and most importantly, completed.

Paul wrote to the Colossians Church and I continue in his prayer that; "we have not ceased to pray for you, asking that you may be filled with the knowledge of his will in all spiritual wisdom and understanding, so as to walk in a manner worthy of the Lord, fully pleasing to him, bearing fruit in every good work and increasing in the knowledge of God. May you be strengthened with all power, according to his glorious might, for all endurance and patience with joy, giving thanks to the Father, who has qualified you to share in the inheritance of the saints in light. He has delivered us from the domain of darkness and transferred us to the kingdom of his beloved Son, in whom we have redemption, the forgiveness of sins." (Colossians 1:9-14).

Walk in the word, be prepared in the Gospel, know the Gospel; know that your path is right and your feet are covered and protected. That is only obtained through study of the word and understanding that is granted by the Spirit through prayer.

SHIELD OF FAITH

Paul then calls us in Ephesians to "take up the shield of faith, with which you can extinguish all the flaming darts of the evil one".

"If you are not firm in faith, you will not be firm at all". Isaiah 7:9

In the Gospels, Jesus healed many. There was not a place it seems, that Jesus went, that as part of his teaching and performing miracles, he healed the sick. But if you read the Gospels closely, and it is noted in each of the 4 Gospels, most that were healed, were healed not by Jesus, but by their faith. Faith in God, faith in his son, an unwavering belief that they would be healed: the Centurion that, "if you would just speak it so", the woman who if she could just touch his clothing. On and on and Jesus repeated, "by your faith, you have been healed".

Jesus promised us, "if you have faith like a grain of a mustard seed, you will say to this mountain, 'Move from here to there,' and it will move, and nothing will be impossible for you." Matthew 17:20

It is our faith that gives us strength and our faith that makes our shield strong.

"So take heart, men, that I have faith in God that it will be exactly as I have been told." Acts 27:25

Keep the faith; stay strong in the faith; renew your faith! "So faith comes through hearing, and hearing through the word of Christ." Romans 10:17

"They were broken off because of their unbelief, (as a branch that does not bear fruit) but you stand fast through faith." Romans 11:20

So then you ask, "How do I have faith, how do I increase faith?" This is a good question and one I have asked myself. We so much want for a huge philosophical answer, we want someone to explain the mysteries of the universe to us, and we want a complex answer to this complex question. I hate to break it to you, but it is simpler than we are willing to admit.

Allow me to explain: You walk to your sink, you turn your faucet and you have faith that water will be there. You do not stop, you do not ask, you do not question; you KNOW that the water will be there. We are so certain that if water doesn't come out, we will repeat the same maneuver multiple times in shock that the water has not come out. Jesus says with less faith than that, we can move mountains.

The problems lie in choice and doubt. When we turn the handle, we see the water, instant results and instant gratification. Unfortunately, we don't control God and rarely does he give us instant gratification. So now were back to choice and doubt.

So ask yourself, honestly, how much do you doubt God? How many times in situations of hardship and trouble have you doubted God's presence? How many times in prayer and study of the Word have thoughts of doubt about your "religion" or your faith entered your mind?

I know that doubt likes to rear its ugly head around me from time to time. God understands this; it is in our flesh to question, to challenge, to seek proof. Conquering this involves just a few simple yet challenging steps.

First is to acknowledge that you have doubt, it's ok, the world may condemn you but your Father will praise your courage! Now that you have acknowledged that you have a weakness, it is about realizing and understanding that it is now about a choice; to simply choose to have doubt, or to choose to have faith. It is that simple, it is we as human beings, under the sins of our flesh, under the pressures of the world that complicate this, but it is as simple as training yourself to CHOOSE to have faith over doubt.

Now again, this does involve training. We have created in ourselves the reflexive response to question and to doubt, it is only through training, study and prayer that a new reflex of faith can begin to enter our lives as we slowly train ourselves to ignore doubt.

And last, you must acknowledge that you cannot go through this training without professional help. You must also acknowledge that it is not in you to handle this on your own and you MUST take it to the feet of Jesus and ask for His help and guidance. The world is too much for all of us and we must always acknowledge that without the help of God the Father, His Son Jesus Christ and the Holy Spirit, WE WILL FAIL!

As simple as I have made it sound, I haven't heard of any mountains being relocated on this planet anywhere, but I have seen spiritual mountains turned to piles of dust through a simple act of faith. So stay in prayer, stay strong in your faith and keep your shield at the ready. For with everything we have said here, know this, the flaming darts of the enemy are already in flight and headed in your direction.

HELMET OF SALVATION

I guess, before I start talking about salvation or the "helmet of salvation", let's define it. Salvation is defined as one; the preservation or deliverance from destruction, difficulty or evil. Christians define salvation as deliverance from the power or penalty of sin. When David had been delivered from his enemies, he sang out: "The Lord is my rock and my fortress and my deliverer, my God, my rock, in whom I take refuge, my shield and the horn of my salvation, my stronghold and my refuge, my savior; you save me from violence. I call upon the Lord who is worthy to be praised, and I am saved from my enemies." 2 Samuel 22:2-4

Jesus came into this world to simply deliver us from the penalty of sin. The price was high, the cost was great, the penalty . . . . paid! Through simply accepting this completely free gift, our salvation is guaranteed. Throughout the bible, God our Father has given salvation, no matter what the challenge, no matter how great the battle, no matter what our *perceived* risk or cost, our salvation is guaranteed.

"Out of my distress I called on the Lord; the Lord answered me and set me free. The Lord is on my side; I will not fear. What can man do to me? The Lord is on my side as my helper; I shall look in triumph on those who hate me." Psalms 118: 5-7

"Be strong and courageous. Do not fear or be in dread of them, for it is the Lord your God who goes with you. He will not leave you or forsake you." Deuteronomy 31:6

So what is Paul saying in wearing a helmet of salvation. I believe that what he is telling us, that we should know, I mean **KNOW**, is that in our minds we need to know that God has already granted us victory. Salvation over our enemies, salvation in our eternity, our salvation from sin, our salvation from death; we need to *know* that it is done, salvation . . . granted!

Have you ever recorded a televised sporting event and then someone tell you the result before you have watched it? Have you ever had someone tell you the ending to a movie, or a book, before you have had a chance to see it or read it? The mystery is gone, the suspense, the anticipation, all taken out of the equation. You may still indulge in the event, however, knowing the ending takes away the suspense, the worry of what will happen next!

What Paul is saying is we need to put on the knowledge or the helmet of our known salvation. Is life still a battle, yes! 1 Timothy 6th chapter tells us to fight the good fight, but Paul reminds us that the movie is over, the book has been written, and the ending is known and WE HAVE WON! (Pause for effect!)

It kind of takes the fear right out of the battle when you know the results beforehand, doesn't it?! The helmet of salvation; the knowledge of salvation; known results, known ending, known victory.

"The Lord is my light and my salvation; whom shall I fear? The Lord is the stronghold of my life, of whom shall I be afraid?" Psalms 27:1

SWORD OF THE SPIRIT

Paul finishes in his description of our Armor of God with; "Sword of the spirit, which is the Word of GOD." (Ephesians 6:17) You may have noticed, and so have I, that with our Armor, this is the only offensive tool noted by Paul. Now the Roman soldier in Paul's day would have, and carry a variety of weapons. The soldier would carry a broad sword, a half broad sword, daggers, darts, various lengths of spears, a bow and/or a sling; I'm sure I'm missing a couple weapons in there as well.

But Paul felt all we needed was one sword, the sword of the spirit. Not only did he tell us the single weapon we would need to wield, but he gave us the single ingredient for its construction, the Word of GOD. Our sword, our offensive weapon, our tool of attack is quite simply, the Bible. The Bible, written by men who were inspired by the Spirit of God; the literal Word of GOD!

The power of the Word of GOD! The Universe and all it contains was created by the Words of GOD, "Let there be", and there was! GOD spoke, and there was, it doesn't get much simpler, yet any more powerful!

"The grass withers, the flower fades, but the Word of our GOD will stand forever." Isaiah 40:8

GOD our Father has given us, provided for us, His written Word; black and white, there right in front of us, for our study, for our guidance, for our encouragement, for our light. As if that was not enough, he sent his only beloved, begotten Son to spell it out for us!

"In the beginning was the Word, and the Word was with God, and the Word was God. He was in the beginning with God. All things were made through him, and without him was not anything made that was made. In Him was life, and the life was the light of men. The light shines in the darkness, and the darkness has not overcome it." (John 1:1-5)

John was referring to Jesus as the Word! The living, breathing, walking, talking Word of GOD! We have Jesus as our example, as our light, as a living testimony to the Word of GOD!

Our sword; our weapon against the forces of evil, the forces of darkness, against our sinful nature, against our flesh; our sword provided to us through the Word of GOD. Any soldier, any officer of the law, any martial artist will tell you it takes years of intense practice before you can be considered a master of a weapon. How much time have we put into mastering our weapon? How much time have we put into the care of our weapon? How strong is our sword, how sharp is our sword? How well are we able to yield it when we need it, when confronted with our enemies? How well do we know our sword? What is our relationship with our sword, what is our relationship with the Word, what is our relationship with GOD the Father, His son Jesus and His Holy Spirit?

The weapon has been provided to us, it is up to us to learn to use it, to become proficient with it, to know it inside and out!

"For the word of GOD is living and active, sharper than any two-edged sword, piercing to the division of soul and of spirit, of joints and of marrow, and discerning the thoughts and the intentions of the heart." (Hebrews 4:12)

I pray that each one of us takes time to recognize that we are in a very real battle. I pray that we take the time necessary to prepare ourselves for the battle in which we are already engaged. I pray that we continue to stand united and look forward to the day when we will all stand united in celebration of the final victory; victory in and through our Lord and Savior . . . Jesus Christ.

Amen

I WAS THINKING . . .

Do I recognize and acknowledge the spiritual battle in which I am engaged?

Am I prepared for the battle or am I entering the field with tattered, poorly constructed, lazily assembled, or even missing armor?

Does the devil see me as an intimidating, well prepared, bearer of the Armor of GOD; or as an easy target that is ripe for the taking, waiting to be destroyed?

Should I maybe be spending more time and energy on my armor?

FINAL PRAYER

PRAYER FOR SPIRITUAL STRENGTH

For this reason I bow my knees before the Father, from whom every family in heaven and on earth is named, that according to the riches of his glory he may grant you to be strengthened with power through his Spirit in your inner being, so that Christ may dwell in your hearts through faith—that you, being rooted and grounded in love, may have strength to comprehend with all the saints what is the breadth and length and height and depth, and to know the love of Christ that surpasses knowledge, that you may be filled with all the fullness of God.

Now to him who is able to do far more abundantly than all that we ask or think, according to the power at work within us, to him be glory in the church and in Christ Jesus throughout all generations, forever and ever. Amen.

(Ephesians 3:14-21 ESV)

WHO AM I?

I am an earthly sinner and a heavenly saint. (The bible says so.) My life's journey has been the story of the prodigal son. Except my twist has been attempting to see how many times I could turn away from my Heavenly Father and have him still accept me back into His arms and under His grace.

There will be undoubtedly some who have known me in my rebellion and question; "Who does this guy think he is? He has some nerve writing about "Christianity"; I used to party with that guy. If there's a sin, he's committed it!" Those statements would be true and they would be right.

I write because God has placed a need on my heart. And I write to share, with those who are struggling with some of the same issues, the lessons I have learned. I write to share some basic simple truths. Not that I fully understand them or that I am able to walk in them. I too struggle every day to walk in the things that I have written. I have identified the path, not perfected the journey.

I have learned that my Heavenly Father is calling me to a greater understanding and a greater relationship. In that understanding, I now have a powerful desire to share that call with as many as I can. I praise God for His grace and His patience with me. I praise him for the blessings of my beautiful wife and my two awesome sons. And I praise Him—for that I know that as you have read this, your relationship with your Heavenly Father has grown!

Help me in sharing the message that; "Your Father is calling." May God bless you and keep you and may His heart be always on your mind.

-Joseph Kleman

Edwards Brothers Malloy
Oxnard, CA USA
June 18, 2014